THE CHURCH

AND

THE STATE

THE CHURCH AND THE STATE

edited by

Donald Reeves

HODDER AND STOUGHTON
LONDON SYDNEY AUCKLAND TORONTO

British Library Cataloguing in Publication Data

The Church and the state.——(Hodder Christian
  paperbacks)
  1. Church of England   2. Church and state
  ——Church of England
  I. Reeves, Donald
  261.7   BX5157

ISBN 0 340 36137 9

Hodder and Stoughton Editorial Office: 47 Bedford Square, London WC1B 3DP

CONTENTS

INTRODUCTION

Donald Reeves

1 Introduction

by Donald Reeves

The purpose of these seven lectures – given at St. James's Church, Piccadilly in February and March 1983 – was to explore some of the issues around the relationship between the Church and society. The lectures are printed more or less as they were delivered with a few modifications for the sake of clarity. It was not assumed at the time that they were going to be published so in some cases the style is more appropriate for the spoken rather than the written word.

The subject has caught the public's attention in a way which might surprise those who believe the Church's influence and standing is weak. How political should the Church be? Should priests and ministers be identified with particular political parties and pressure groups? The *Sun*, the *Daily Mail*, the *Daily Telegraph* and *The Times* make the most of every opportunity to attack those Church leaders and Church organisations who dare to make some sort of comment about social, economic or political matters. The labels 'trendy', 'do-gooding' and 'left-wing' are certainly rather tired and over-used, but they appear to be the only ones available to attack those who preach a 'social gospel'.

Therefore it was hoped that these lectures, given by distinguished Church leaders and politicians, might shed some light on these contentious issues. But in arranging this series I was acutely aware of the turbulent and disturbed times in which the Church 'functions'. In such a world it is necessary to understand, clarify and perhaps to indicate something of the task, identity and shape of the Church – not least because many observers predict a global situation which will deteriorate rapidly in the next twenty or so years. It is not too much to say that our civilisation is entering a period which is something like the Dark Ages. It is therefore vital to sketch some roles and tasks for the Church which reflect faithfully an awareness in all its complexity of this grim prospect, and which faithfully may respond to the Gospel.

Ronald Higgins, in the introduction to the second edition of his book, *The Seventh Enemy*, provides a telling reminder of the global context:

> We have somehow created a world of profound and increasing inequalities, in which the top third of our fellow men and women live in restless affluence and the bottom third in degrading poverty. It is a world in which absurd expectations, compulsive appetites and human multiplication are exhausting scarce resources and endangering the land, the waters and the atmosphere. It is a world where deprivation and injustice have become so profound and so public that they make even more precarious the balance of nuclear terror which has become the extraordinary and permanent context of our lives. We must prepare ourselves for a world of rapidly mounting confusion and horror. The next twenty-five years, possibly the next ten, are likely to bring starvation to hundreds of millions, and hardship, disaster or war to most of the rest of us. Democracy, where it exists, can have little chance of survival. Nor in the long run can our extravagant urban industrial way of life. The evidence as a whole strongly suggests

that an era of anarchy and widespread suffering is
swiftly coming upon us...
(*The Seventh Enemy*, Hodder and Stoughton, page 12)

These words, and the mountain of evidence provided to
substantiate them, are easily dismissed as unnecessarily
pessimistic and even inaccurate. The forecaster's path is
littered with banana skins. In the 1960s, for example,
when there were around 11½ million cars it was forecast
that by 1983, the number of cars would have trebled to
35 million. It is in fact only around 20 million. Again, for
years many people have predicted the end of the printed
word in the light of the pervasive presence of television
and radio, but the facts are that there is a steady rise in
the sale of books worldwide of between 3 and 4 per cent
in the last twenty years. Moreover, we in Britain in
times of emergency and crisis have always managed to
overcome our problems. It is just a matter of looking on
the bright side, taking initiatives, pulling our collective
selves together – then we shall once again put the Great
back into Britain. Understandably, politicians will not
endorse the scenario of Ronald Higgins or other 'doom-
watchers'. And in the short term, if some of the
prophecies turned out wrong, the overall trends which
Ronald Higgins and others define ring unmistakably
true, even though the time-scale may not always be
accurate.

A visitor to our islands from another planet would see
two nations – one of the South-East and parts of the
West Country relatively prosperous, and another
Britain of the Midlands and the North. The persistence
of poverty and unemployment, the collapsing Welfare
State (and the lack of funds to finance it), racial
discrimination and harassment, the growth of crime and
violence on the streets, the disappearance of voluntary
and community organisations – this catalogue is familiar
to anyone who lives or works in our major cities and

housing estates. The causes of such a state of affairs tain and globally are beyond the scope of this essay, but a felt awareness of these signs of the times with the potential for violence, and for social and political instability demand radical responses of clarity and courage, faith and obedience.

It is easy enough to write that last sentence. It is quite another matter to say precisely what those demands look like in practice given all the ambiguities and inertia of our institutions which fail to attend to these enormous problems. Any grasp of the seriousness of our situation paralyses the will, and freezes the imagination. After all, what is there that you and I can do to make a difference – how can our voices be heard? It is only too easy to be neither hawk, nor dove, let alone wise owls, but ostriches who bury their heads deep in the sand.

It is possible to detect within the Church not just an ostrich-like response, but also one of fear and confusion. Some feel betrayed by the Church: they look to it as the one unchanging institution in a world of much change (even if they themselves are not actively involved as church-goers). Times of uncertainty generate nostalgia and sentiment, and if the Church does not offer that consolation then yet another landmark is destroyed. Moreover in times of uncertainty when much is at stake, governments look to the institutions of religion to bless their actions and provide a moral basis. And if the Church responds hesitatingly or ambiguously or con-trary to public expectation, anger and subtle harassment of Christians will begin. When fear reigns, then clarity and courage, faith and obedience are nowhere to be seen. As the debate about the Church's involvement in the world's affairs grows, so it is possible to detect a more thought-out response, which at root is an expression of fear. It goes something like this:

> Men and women are prone to do evil; they are readily agents of wickedness and therefore of

suffering. They are motivated by self-interest. We live in a fallen, flawed and corrupt world caused by our extraordinary capacity to sin. Governments are necessary, particularly strong aggressive governments; they prevent us from destroying one another. There is little that each of us can do except undertake small acts of charity and neighbourliness as they come our way. It may well be that through our own stupidity we shall destroy much of this planet, particularly if we allow ourselves to respond feebly to our enemy. If that is so, so be it. The task of the Church and of its ministers is to prepare our souls for the life beyond the grave – through the salvation offered to us on the Cross. We pray and study the scriptures and expect the clergy to teach us to pray and study better. We avail ourselves of the sacraments of the Church.

That is, of course, a caricature. Such views are rarely expressed so blatantly. Yet it is difficult to account for the hostility which greets the reports and pronouncements of the Churches on social matters unless it springs from such attitudes and understanding of religious belief and practice. They are deeply held. They lie dormant until they are disturbed. They play on the fears aroused by a sense of the scale of the problems before us. They collude with the individualism and privatising of our values. The cynicism with which politicians are regarded (as in the popular television series *Yes Minister*) is a telling indication of how politics and public affairs seem to intrude on the 'peace' which we try to create within our own personal and domestic circles. The way to change the world for peace and justice, so the argument goes, is just to change our hearts. Something called 'society' out there attempts to thwart whatever we can discover of peace and hope.

For those who perceive their religion in some such way, the church with its doors locked is an appropriate

13

sign. The church building is used only for those who are 'in the know'. It is not available for those searching for faith or those who see churches as having a place in the life of the neighbourhood. The locked church encourages the notion of the parish as the thirty or forty or seventy or whatever who come together to worship. But, at least within the tradition of the Church of England, the parish is primarily the neighbourhood which the Church community, building and parson are there to serve. Even the Alternative Service Book can exclude those who are not in the know, through its insistence on maximum participation and its bald statements to which everyone must assent – 'The Lord is here' or 'We are the Body of Christ'. What room is there in our churches today for those with questioning and doubting hearts? Even house meetings and small groups, which are so often encouraging signs of new life, degenerate all too easily into inwardness or parochialism. The 'locked church' mentality resists addressing the world: professional clergymen and those in specialist ministries may feel more adequate and fulfilled in being contentious, but, so this analysis goes, lay men and women need a haven of peace and quiet, where comfort and consolation are provided, and a community where aggravation and conflict are as far as possible avoided.

What is so inadequate about these popular perceptions of Christian belief and practice is that all the meaning and content of the Christian faith have been removed. Since Christianity has been reduced to a matter of personal and private concern, it loses any sort of interest for the world at large. It is just there for the few who happen to like that sort of thing. In its separation of the 'spiritual' from everything else, it would hardly appear incongruous for the commandant of Auschwitz to attend Church Sunday by Sunday! In remembering the potential for evil and wickedness, so is forgotten the potential for good and the fact that men and women are born in the image of God. In emphasising the corruption inherent in our nature, so we ignore that God is our faithful Creator, and part of our responsibility and response to God's creating and sustaining energy is that we are to be the trustees of our planet.

In reducing the practice of Christianity to the performance of spiritual exercises in preparation for the life hereafter, the historical basis of the ministry of Jesus is forgotten; the teachings and demonstrations of the Kingdom are ignored. Paul's teachings about the Church as the Body of Christ are bypassed. The hope which the future holds both now and beyond death, as declared in the Resurrection, has no place. The great themes of redemption and salvation – which tell of the liberation and renewal of individuals, societies and the entire cosmos – are reduced to private moments of comfort and uplift.

Such a shrunken view of Christianity has nothing to offer a battered world. Indifference and contempt are a sufficient response. But it is possible to detect an altogether different response expressed most powerfully by the Archbishop of York, John Habgood, in his book *Church and Nation in a Secular Age*, and by Professor Chadwick in his lecture. The Archbishop perceives the signs of the times as just the opportunity for the national established Church of England to wake up to its responsibilities and, to put it crudely, provide the cement for a building which is developing many faults in its ancient structure. The Archbishop quotes a previous Archbishop of Canterbury, Cosmo Lang, who, in a speech in the House of Lords on the subject of the Church in Wales, asked:

Whether in the public corporate life of the nation there is to be any assertion at all of its religious beliefs, of its acknowledgement of the Almighty God, of its concern with the religious life of the people . . . The State has an organic unity of spirit of its own, and that character and spirit are built up by tradition and association running far back into the past. Its life is expressed not only by the policies and pursuits of the present, but also by a sort of subconscious continuity which endures and profoundly affects the character of each generation of citizens who enter within it. The question before us . . . is whether just there in that inward region of the national life where anything that can be called its unity and character is expressed, there is or is not to be this witness to some ultimate sanction to which the nation looks, some ultimate ideal it proposes. It is in our judgment a very serious thing for a state to take out of that corporate heart of its life any acknowledgement at all of its concern with religion.

(Page 101 in *Church and Nation in a Secular Age* by John Habgood; Darton, Longman and Todd. Cited in Edward Norman's *Church and Society in England*, page 278)

That long quotation is, as the Archbishop remarks, a powerful argument for the continuing 'establishment' of the Church – not for the Church's sake but for the good of the nation. The question is whether this relationship between Church and State is real enough to provide that 'unity' which certainly is needed now more than at any other time.

In 1913, when Archbishop Lang said those words, the Church of England was already weak in influence, and since then its influence has declined considerably. Britain is a multiracial and multifaith society. Indifference to institutional religion is marked by the decline of numbers who attend Church. Certainly Archbishop Lang's defence of the establishment is powerful and convincing; and as our predicament becomes more intractable, and as the social fabric shows increasing signs of stress, it is probable that many will join the Archbishop of York in defending the establishment and using the opportunities that an established Church offers to help create a more stable and just society. (The contrary view about the establishment of the Church of England, expressed in the Bishop of Kensington's and Tony Benn's lectures, is also to be found in *Church and Nation* by Peter Cornwell [Basil Blackwell].)

But to look to the Church of England to be the national Church for England is sadly too late in the day.

Close identification of the Church with the State is an illusion. Bishops in the House of Lords, and State occasions serve to reinforce this illusion. It is difficult to discover any evidence that the established Church is meeting the role Archbishop Lang hoped for it. Moreover the nation is too divided for the Church to provide that unity and cement, since most of its presence and ministry is with the privileged. Had, for example, the Church of England taken seriously its responsibilities as the Church for the nation then it certainly would not have waited until now (when it is almost too late) to establish an Archbishop's Commission on the Church in the Inner Cities.

No doubt the response to Archbishop Lang's case depends in part where you stand. Clergy who have worked in housing estates and inner city areas – where most of the population still live – know that those who live in these areas have no particular expectation of the Church of England, because it is the established Church. It does not feature in the consciousness and imaginations of working-class men and women. In some country towns the vicar of the parish church by right and by custom has some position in the committees and councils of the neighbourhood. But in Walsall, or Bermondsey, Hackney or Sunderland, he will have to earn his place. Churches in these areas are tiny, frail communities (though often of great faith and hope and with much to teach the rest of us about endurance). They are frequently experienced as alien and insensitive and even oppressive by those whom they come to serve.

Moreover the knowledge that the Church of England is somehow a Church for the nation does not always help the long process of nurturing a local ministry.

As the vicar of a vast South London housing estate, I remember visiting several families who were asking for baptism for their children at the time of the enthronement of Lord Coggan as Archbishop of Canterbury. The service had been televised. It was a natural talking point. Two of the families independently made the same point: 'Well, he lives in a palace, doesn't he?' It was pointless for me to explain that the Archbishop and his wife led a very simple life and that as Archbishop he needed premises for offices and entertainment. Their response indicated a gulf: the Church was not for them. They felt and knew instinctively that their local parish church (built at the same time as the rest of the estate) was not theirs in the same way as, say, the Working Men's Club, the Horticultural Society or even the local pubs and meeting places. The Church for them was a reminder of a class-divided society, and for those of us responsible for the ministry there it seemed as if we were managing a colonial outpost controlled and administered by a central organisation which knew little or nothing of its territories.

There is no accepted understanding of the Church's position in our society. There has always been and will always be differing views and different practices. The difficulty with analyses and critiques (and these sketches are of course no way exhaustive) is that any question about what can be done leads to the inevitable answer 'Not much'. There is a built-in determinism and conservatism about some sorts of description which do not allow for something new to break in and alter the perspective so that a new practice can emerge. But sociological perspectives are not definitive. Theological perspectives fashioned in part by the content of Church and society ultimately transcend social or political limitations.

So where does the Word of God break in?

It could be that, properly apprehended and grasped, the fear of our situation offers a last chance which could turn out to be the best chance. Granted that the churches are as weak as I have indicated, then is not their very weakness a chance for them both to own the fear of the coming Dark Ages and also to be faithful to the Gospel? For now our churches have nothing to lose, and everything to gain.

And it is to the nature of the identity of the Church in our turbulent society that some thought has to be given. Difficult times tempt absolute and simple solutions; it is only too easy to parade some version of fundamentalism which ignores the realities and contradictions of the institutional life of the Church.

But the starting point is clear. It is clear and radical. It is nothing less than the churches' discovering their vocation as those who proclaim God's judgment on the world, and summon us to repentance. Judgment is a recognition that God – who visits our perverse hearts and all those institutions and governments which bruise, enslave, oppress and silence men and women – is close to us. The apprehension of the closeness of God invites repentance and a reformation of the churches. Among the tangled business of politics, power and public affairs (which altogether determine our future), the unique role of the Church is its strange, unwelcome and persistent vocation to proclaim repentance. It will be a tiny voice among many others. But it is inescapable as we enter a time of widespread suffering. The Church's vocation, however faithfully lived, will not itself stem that tide. There is no guarantee that renewed faithfulness in these matters will bring 'success' (whatever that may be), because our lives in this sense are in the hands of God. But in line with the tradition of the prophets and of the apocalyptic tradition, and supremely in the ministry of Jesus, the message is the same: 'Except ye repent, we shall all perish'.

It is this voice which Victor de Waal in his lecture identifies as 'critical solidarity' and which will, inevitably, displease authorities and powers in Church and State.

The sense of the closeness of God in judgment and also in promise calls for nothing less than a reformation of the churches. In difficult times, they need to provide some manifestation or 'demonstration' of this apprehension of the knowledge of God. Repentance, individually and corporately, means undergoing a process of cleansing and purging.

If a new sense of the Gospel calls us to bother about those least able to help themselves, then every effort has to be made to deploy our resources of time, energy and money to those areas and classes which are most deprived and disadvantaged.

If a new sense of the Gospel calls us to promote a society where the dignity of each is recognised, then, in the life of the Church, everything that can be done must be done to remove the separation between women and men, clergy and laity.

If a new sense of the Gospel calls us to support those who have been bruised and enslaved and ignored, then, in the life of the Church, everything that can be done has to be done to ensure that their voices are heard in the councils of the churches.

If a new sense of the Gospel calls us to recognise the establishing of just relationships in our society or Church, then the churches have to discover how to stand critically and clearly in relationship to those classes and institutions which are the chief causes of poverty.

The sharing, the emptying, the giving away of resources individually and corporately is one of the signs of a Church repentant and aware of the closeness of God. What prevents us from movement in these directions is the lack of knowledge and experience of God – who comes to us in judgment and in hope. Where this begins to happen, so a new understanding of the fellowship of the Holy Spirit blossoms. The trials and conflicts of Christian communities trying to be faithful compel a new corporate sense of the Church, for it is only from one another that true fellowship is realised. The prayer of Christians, separately and together, is inescapable, for it is in prayer that we, with the eyes of God as revealed in Christ, seek to see the suffering and whatever is there by way of Grace in the world. In the worship of the Church, the Easter faith is rehearsed, celebrated and experienced as a hope which, against all hope, offers faith in a hopeless world and reminds us that the future before us is open – even beyond the gates of death.

THE CHURCH AND POLITICS

Shirley Williams

2 The Church and Politics

Shirley Williams

This is a strange topic to ask a politician to speak about, for it's been a century since the question of the establishment or disestablishment of the Church of England, or the Church in Wales, or the Church in Ireland was near the centre of the political agenda.

In Britain we have got an established Church. The Queen is the head of the Church; the Prime Minister has a very substantial say in who becomes a bishop of the Church; and the Church itself is a naturally Pauline Church – by which I mean its instinct is to uphold the established order. Through education, in particular, the Church and the State are intermingled in England and Wales. Most people don't know the complexities of the 1944 Education Act, which remains the foundation of the educational system, but the Education Act lays down a commitment by the State to support Church schools of one kind or another: Anglican schools, Roman Catholic schools and a small number of orthodox Jewish schools.

So there is a very close interrelationship between the Church and the State in Britain; it has had the effect in the past that the Church has been, and has been seen to be, a part of the established order of things. When you go into most parish churches you see the flags of regiments; when you attend Armistice Day ceremonies they are often a patriotic celebration of the relationship between the Church and the country; until the last twenty or thirty years, vicars were often the voice of the established order in whatever parish they happened to be.

If I take my own Church, the Roman Catholic Church, this is also true – or has been true – of its relationship to the secular State. There have been concordats between the Vatican and various European and Latin American countries. There is an uneasy recognition of the Church's role in Poland; the Communist government recognises that the Church is so strong there that some *modus vivendi* is essential. If the Church stands aside from political issues, it abdicates its role as a moral guide and leader. Yet if the Church is directly identified with any one political party, then a large part of the body of the Church, its members, will be offended and even to some extent resentful, because in a democracy individual electors do not think that the Churches should tell them how they ought to vote. Most of you would be shocked if, at the next election, the Rector of St. James's, Piccadilly, was to get up in the pulpit and tell you in precise terms how you ought to vote, for which party and for which candidates. That's something we associate with more remote areas of Western Europe where the priest may have told his parishioners to vote Christian Democrat; priests nowadays are very reluctant to do that.

How does the Church square this dilemma? Let's begin with the extreme case. In the extreme case where the State embodies and espouses values which are anti-Christian, the Church cannot be associated directly with the State and its establishment. I suppose the obvious examples of this were the relationships of the Lutheran Church and the Catholic Church with the German State under Hitler and with the Italian State under Mussolini. There was a concordat between the Catholic Church and Mussolini's Italy. There was some cooperation in the early period of Nazism between the Chancellor, Adolf

Hitler, and the Lutheran Church which was the State Church of Germany. The Churches were, therefore, associating with States which by their very philosophy and values could only be described as profoundly anti-Christian because, in the last analysis, the doctrine of Nazism is a doctrine of a master race and, therefore, cannot be compatible with the concept of the infinite value of every individual human being, whatever his or her religion, race, nation or origin.

At the present time the nearest analogy is the relationship between the Russian Orthodox Church, which has always been an established Church, a Church which is close to the institutions of the State, and the Soviet State, which is by definition a State which regards Christianity as a heresy and a deliberate fraud upon the people. The relationship between the Orthodox Church and Communist State is a very difficult relationship in which the Orthodox are becoming more and more a separate order outside the structure of the State and are seen by the State as incompatible with its own values and standards.

Let me move away now from extreme cases, the case of States which are anti-Christian by definition, and turn instead to our own secular domestic States. Historically and traditionally, the Church has always been expected to take a role on a very limited number of issues that come before the politicians and Parliament. Those issues are defined as 'moral issues' and are particularly concerned with marriage, the family and sexual morality. On issues concerned with pornography, abortion and divorce, the legislators expect there to be a Church position and it's never been regarded as controversial for the Church to take up a straight-forward and strong position in such areas.

I think that this has to some extent damaged the Churches, not because of their stand on morality, but because such issues have been seen often as the only moral issues on which the Church has the right to speak.

It has not been regarded as controversial for the Churches to be heard on issues concerning personal conduct in fields like gambling or alcoholism or the use of drugs. It's when the Churches begin to move into the wider political issues that people say it is no part of the Churches' business to get mixed up with these issues. The paradox is that those very politicians who most resent the Church taking a stand on our relations with the Third World or on defence, or on issues concerning, for example, the individual rights of immigrants, are often the very politicians who welcome the Church's voice on sexual morality.

Let us be quite blunt about it – on the left wing the voice of the Church in relation to the Third World, race relations, immigration and so forth is welcome; the voice of the Church on individual morality is not welcome. On the right wing the voice of the Church on peace, on Third World issues, on race relations or on immigration is not welcome. Therefore the Church is just about in the right position, because by having found its voice again it has succeeded in offending just about everybody. If one goes back to the New Testament, and the teachings and lessons of Christ, that is where He expected us to be. He it was, after all, who did not reach an agreeable compromise with the Philistines or the Saducees, or the money-changers in the Temple, but was regarded by all of them as an outsider, a dissenter and a non-conformist. So let me take several issues and look at what might be the stand that the Churches take or, perhaps more precisely, the stand that Christians take, and find out who is offended and who isn't.

On the question of personal morality, the Church has something to say because human relations affect other human beings and can harm them or benefit them. The Church has to pick its way between the need for tolerance of the difference in human behaviour and the need to speak out openly and loudly about forms of exploitation of human beings. Few of us would now support the idea that was pursued for many centuries of listing books forbidden to the faithful. Yet one can believe that certain forms of pornography should be attacked, not so much because they are pornography, as because they devalue the human being into nothing more than a body without either a heart, a mind or a soul. Some sorts of pornography which suggest that women are simply instruments or animals are deeply offensive for this reason. Pornography is essentially dehumanising.

But if pornography is dehumanising, then let me say equally strongly that the way we treat prisoners in our prisons is also profoundly dehumanising. Having three adult men pushed together in a tiny cell in which there's hardly room to turn around, 'slopping out' because as a community we don't find the money to provide them with lavatories, is a form of degradation not very different from pornography because it is essentially dehumanising human beings. We should speak out against the second just as strongly as against the first. Yet again the paradox is that being against pornography is considered right-wing and being in favour of reforming prison conditions is considered left-wing. It seems to me that the Christian should stand for both because he or she is, as a principle, against the dehumanising of individuals.

Let me take another example of an interesting paradox. On the whole it has been on the right of politics that voices have been raised against abortion. But if one does believe that each human life, including human life in the womb, is sacred, then how about capital punishment? Isn't capital punishment making a judgment about what happens to an individual human being, and assuming that redemption is impossible. Is it for human beings to say that another human being cannot be redeemed and therefore to declare their judicial ending? To me it has always seemed that accepting the value of each potential human life can't stop short when it gets to the issue of capital punishment, because that is of a piece with the view that the individual human being has the right to life. Yet again, as you will see, these issues have been both left-wing and right-wing issues.

Let me take another one. There is something wholly wrong about the House of Commons spending five hours debating the question of whether or not Britain is prepared to accept the husbands of British citizens who happen to be brown or black. The immigration rules contradict most of the values we have been taught as Christians to believe in. It is not for us to say that British citizens may not marry because the State finds it objectionable that they should wish to marry someone who happens to be living in some other country and who wishes to come to this country, just because they are not British citizens.

Some of the ways in which we are beginning to invade the privacy of individual human beings should be the subject of debate by Church members. I think we should be much more worried than we are about the impact on the individual of the computerisation of Government records, police records, National Health records and all the rest of it. I heard on the radio this morning that it's estimated that the names of 300,000 people who are not yet settled in this country are on computer because they are said in some way to have offended the Home Office's immigration rules. But, as John Donne said a long time ago, 'no man is an island'. And as Dietrich Bonhoeffer said: 'First they came for the Jews and I was not a Jew; then they came for the Socialists and I was not a Socialist; then they came for the trade unionists and I was not a trade unionist; and then there was no one left, and they came for me.'

The individual liberty frontiers are defined by what happens to the least favoured individual, not to the most favoured individual. That's why what matters are the computer records of the mentally handicapped and their treatment; the rules that deal with people who want to visit their relations in Britain and are stopped at the airport because they can't explain in bureaucratic language why they want to do so; it is the treatment of prisoners and vagrants, society's unwanted. These are what determine the values and standards of a society. The Churches should worry now about the computer-isation of our society, and should raise strong voices calling for the protection of individuals' privacy, their rights of choice and their free will as individual creatures of God.

In politics this means concern with the nuts and bolts of things like the access of individuals to computer records, the construction of checks and balances between one set of computers and another, of things like making sure that nobody can have information about him or her transferred to an employer or a tax authority or a social worker without his or her permission or the permission of his or her guardian.

I turn next to international affairs, because it seems to me inescapable for the Churches to speak out about an essential Christian doctrine: the obligation of the rich towards the poor. Whether one turns to the story of the Good Samaritan or to what Christ said about the eye of the needle and the rich man, or indeed more recently towards what has been said by Christians and others in respect of the Brandt Commission and the work of bodies like Christian Aid, it is clear that both within our own society and within the larger international society Christians cannot pretend that there are no obligations that flow from possessing more than other people.

Within our own society that means that we have obligations to make sure that there is no poverty so grave that our fellow human beings undergo avoidable suffering. With all its faults, the Welfare State embodies the central concept that we are members one of another. It embodies in social terms the concept of the good neighbour; that we do look after the sick, the disabled, the elderly, those who cannot look after themselves.

31

But the Welfare State is seen largely in national terms. We think about our own Welfare State, what we have in England, in Holland, in Germany or in France, and we have become defensive and territorial about it. When we look at the world as a whole then the concept that operates there is the concept of Victorian charity. It is the concept of doling out aid, of giving from our benevolence and goodwill some small crumbs to those who are suffering in other parts of the world – and God knows they are suffering: people are absolutely destitute in places like Uganda, Cambodia and Ethiopia; they move in an inchoate and disordered way in desperate pursuit of food, or water or security. It can't have escaped your notice that the number of these disordered population movements, of people desperately trying to escape from some part of the world that is literally collapsing around them to some other place that looks more secure, is beginning to destabilise the world. If it is allowed to continue, it will destabilise us, as surely as it has already destabilised Cambodia and Vietnam, Ethiopia and Somalia, Uganda and Northern Kenya and, most recently, Lebanon – which, twenty years ago, was just as prosperous as Britain was in the 1960s.

So we have for our own sakes, as well as for reasons of Christian duty, to move from Victorian charity towards an ordered form of help which is what the Welfare State is supposed to be. That is what the first and second Brandt Commissions were addressing themselves to; an attempt to strengthen an international structure based upon bodies like the World Bank and the International Monetary Fund, but also based upon a new initiative which would enable the countries of the world to create a new partnership between the unemployed rich and the unfed, unsupplied poor. When you stop to think for just a moment about the electric effect that the Marshall Plan had on Europe after the war, when American capacity was harnessed to the needs of what was then a continent on its knees, one can begin to see that the grand vision isn't just a vision; it is something that has been put into practice within the living memory of those who are middle-aged or elderly.

I turn finally to two other issues. The first of those issues which must leap to everybody's mind is the issue of war and peace. There are, of course, grounds for a discussion about the best way to get a lasting peace. The unilateralists and the multilateralists have their argument about whether it is the unilateral path of example or the multilateral path of negotiation that will lead us to a lasting peace. My own belief is that the path of multilateralism is more likely to do so because I don't believe any of the superpowers would follow the example of unilateralism. Indeed, both Andropov and Reagan have made this absolutely clear.

But this doesn't permit us to escape from the moral dilemma, because the clear moral objective by which anybody who talks about peace must be judged is what priority they give to it. The women of Greenham Common are unilateralists; therefore I don't agree with their political judgment. But they have their priorities right because they regard peace as a priority so overwhelming that it must replace their own comfort and the pattern of their own lives. I wish that governments, including our own, gave to the pursuit of disarmament the same degree of priority. Those of us who are multilateralists can only begin to justify our case if we bend every nerve and every effort towards the achievement of a negotiated reduction of arms and an end to the arms race.

The wish by both Britain and France, Socialist France and Conservative Britain, to keep their own nuclear weapons out of any negotiation is, in my view, wrong if the inclusion of the British and French deterrent within negotiations could bring the possibility of success one iota nearer. We cannot stand on the sidelines and address the United States and the Soviet Union on the necessity of agreeing to a reduction in their own nuclear weapons if we, the British, and we, the French, don't want to accept any reduction in our own arms.

It surely must be becoming more and more clear to all of us that our amazing technological and scientific capacity, the vast potential of the human brain, is out of symmetry with the *moral* development of human beings. We have immense capacity for invention, for destruction, for creation, and we have hardly a clue how to use those powers, to what end and for what purpose.

All of us must be aware that we are pushing the environment of our planet and its natural resources to the limits of what they can stand; already we are beginning to see the threats to the fragile ecology of the planet upon which we live. As desecration grows, as supplies of fresh water become rarer, as with every year that passes more and more arable acres cease to be cultivated, it is we who must ask ourselves how we have used the heritage of nature and of intellect that God has given us. The answer is that we have misused it appallingly. Somehow over the next thirty or forty years we have got to balance our immense intellectual and economic resources with some development of our moral sense. When one looks from the aggressive, competitive, fast-running West to the more peaceful and eternal philosophies of Asia, one can see how the world has become unsynchronised, even one hemisphere with another.

I was delighted that the Churches have once again found their voice. I think it's excellent that the Archbishop of Canterbury should now be a controversial figure, because the only way the Churches will be listened to is if, sometimes, they say things we do not want to hear. There are things we don't want to hear because they embarrass us as politicians. There are things the Prime Minister doesn't want to hear because it embarrasses her as a politician; there are things that Neil Kinnock doesn't want to hear – but we need to be made to listen; the Churches need to be in the eye of the storm. Increasingly the Archbishop of Canterbury and his fellow bishops, the Pope and his fellow cardinals, are saying things that people have to listen to, though they may not want to hear.

The task of the Churches is to bear witness to the teaching of Christ; that teaching is as valid and as much in conflict with the established values of secular society as when it was first uttered 2,000 years ago.

THE LINK BETWEEN CHURCH AND STATE

Owen Chadwick

3 The Link between Church and State

by Owen Chadwick

The problem of today stems from December 1927. In about 1900 the House of Commons had demanded that the Church put her house in order, e.g., restrain extreme forms of ritual. A commission was appointed to see how this was to be done. And after a world war and about 25 years, the organs of the Church, the Church Assembly and the Convocations and the Bishops, sent to Parliament a draft of a new Prayer Book. This, to everyone's surprise, was passed by the House of Lords comfortably; and on December 14th, 1927 it was thrown out by a majority in the House of Commons.

It was not so much the throwing out of the new Prayer Book of 1927 as the way in which it was thrown out. A majority of the English Members of Parliament voted in favour of the new Prayer Book and the Prayer Book was thrown out by the votes of Scottish, Irish and Welsh MPs. And in particular the MP for Paisley, who was a man called Rosslyn Mitchell, and rather a theosophist, and not frequent in the House of Commons, made a fierce speech; if you read it now you cannot understand how it could sway respectable men and women. It was a rant worthy of the seventeenth century. But all the evidence is that Rosslyn Mitchell's speech, which was contemptible, swayed votes in that debate in the House of Commons.

It had become evident, over a hundred years, that the House of Commons was not a suitable organ for the government of a Church. This was made infinitely plain in December 1927. From about 1850 rival organs of government for the established Church of England had been built. The Convocations of Canterbury and of York contained clergy only, and therefore were unsuitable in the long run for representative assemblies. In the 1880s and 90s these Convocations took to themselves a body of laymen called, at first, the House of Laymen. From about 1904/5 the laymen and the clergy of the Convocations met together in what came to be called the Represent-ative Church Council, and this became the Church Assembly – which is the immediate father of the General Synod which meets today. After what happened on December 14th, 1927 some kind of synod for governing the Church was absolutely indispensable.

All assemblies for discussion have demerits. The human race has foolish men as well as wise men and foolish women as well as wise women. And all representative assemblies, not excluding the House of Commons, are not so representative as they look. As forms of government, all such societies, all assemblies, have demerits as well as merits.

We have in Britain a very interesting historical situation, a very historic Church, with relations of an intimate kind with the State, and which has come in modern times to develop its own independent organs of government, its makers of liturgy, drafters of doctrine and the like. The Church is embedded into the history of the British people and on the whole the British people like it to be so. They think of the long tradition and grandeur of the English religious tradition. They know that they have a Church as old as the English people, which helped to create the English people out of little kingdoms and tribes, and grew as a *national* Church – not as a Church of the elect, drawing holy and devout men out of society, but as a Church trying to make its impact upon the whole of society.

The danger of such a national idea of religion was, and is, worldliness. The more you go out into society the more your clergy, the more your laity, have the danger of being swamped by the materialism of the society in which they live. But still, although worldliness might be said to be a danger in this type of tradition, it has also the glory of outgoingness. Too much mixtures with the world may be bad but it is so bad as too little mixture with the world.

I go on holiday to the Norfolk coast and enjoy the local bar, which is otherwise occupied by workers in agriculture or coastguards or by fishermen, or sometimes by someone in the building trade. Most of them would hardly dream of going to church unless one of their colleagues dies or occasionally for the British Legion or for a marriage. Nevertheless, this group of British workers watches its church with lively interest, is proud of it and would be horrified if anyone suggested that you knock it down, and occasionally they are extremely generous to it. Why should anybody like to disturb such a heritage?

We see in this country a general diffused, inarticulate assent to Christianity as an ideal in the body of the nation, by people participating in Christian search and Christian service, by people participating in services in the church at birth or at marriage or death. And so far as they want to relate their lives to a wider framework than the material existence, they seek to relate it to an eternity which is understood through the Church.

There are those who regard this, which is called diffused Christianity, with contempt. I cannot understand why. They must be bigoted and narrow-minded men and women who regard such diffused Christianity with scorn, who think that you can only be a Christian if you accept every line of the Athanasian creed. We ought

41

to regard this tradition in Britain not with contempt but with gratitude. You may think religiosity inadequate. You may think that some of this is much too vague to be powerful on anybody's conscience. But it is a most precious inheritance and affects the moral ideals of the society in which we live. I am convinced that the Church, if it were to despise the inarticulate feeling among many of our people that they share in the Christian religion, would be missing a great opportunity, which is *the* great opportunity among all the Churches. It would be a failure of goodwill and a failure in faith.

I turn to the necessary friction. A Church which wants the chaplain to bless whatever is done by the government in power would not be much of a Church. The Church must be itself. It must live its own life in the service of its own Master. It ought never to tell people, 'Nobody must vote Conservative'; it ought never to tell people, 'Nobody must vote Labour', because for the Church, humanity is not a category. The humanity in which the Church is dealing is always of the individual: political parties have good Christians and worse Christians, good men and less good men of every kind.

The Church may denounce, let us say, the theory of class warfare as immoral, and that will have political implications. It may denounce the theory of racial obsessive nationalism as immoral, and that will have political overtones. The Church cannot be said to be above politics. But it is never partisan. It is not dealing in political parties; it is dealing in individual members of political parties and therefore in a necessity of friction.

Most archbishops of Canterbury during this century have had strong arguments with the government in power. The leaders of the Church have a duty to say what they feel about the moral issues of the day. Argument at least, conflict perhaps, is inevitable. The churchman asks himself, what is right by the law of God? The statesman asks himself, what is the least harmful thing that I can do in this impossible situation?

The man of politics sometimes accuses the churchman of an impracticable idealism. The churchman sometimes wonders whether the line which the politician treads is still fully moral.

The most difficult, perhaps, of the links is under discussion. The Church of England has her liberties: she has freedom of worship, she has freedom of choice of persons, she has more freedom over property than is available to other denominations. Who has an interest in bishops? The parishes, of course. The children who come to be confirmed have an interest in bishops. The ordinands to be trained as clergymen have an interest in bishops. The clergy and their problems, they have an interest in bishops. But the history of our nation also says that the nation has an interest in bishops.

In the old universities of this country and of Scotland, the oldest professorships are still filled by the Crown. And the regius professorships at Oxford and Cambridge and several Scottish universities have this remarkable feature about them. Those who hold them are given a primacy of honour in their university. They are not usually given any more power but they are given a primacy of honour because they are the choice of the Queen. A bishop chosen only by a committee in a diocese or even by a committee of several dioceses might be a very good man, but he would not in any way be sent by the Queen and therefore he would not have that primacy of honour which is attached to a regius chair.

The modern system is good, that when the Prime Minister nominates to the Queen somebody for election to a see, the choice of names has been vetted by good men who know about these things in the Church. But the nation as well as the Church has an interest in who are the leaders of the Church. Historically that has always been so. No other system of appointing bishops has prevailed for long either in our Church or in any other.

I perceive a dangerous desire within the Church to kill

itself. Who has an interest in our Prayer Book and our liturgy? Is it only those who go to church every Sunday? Or are there others? The new Prayer Book, the Alternative Service Book of 1980, is a fine book in nearly all its parts. I am grateful to the creators of that book for what they did, especially its work in all the minor offices which are not minor, including great moments of life like marriages and funerals. But certain aspects and attitudes are wrong for any church in our day. Last Sunday was Quinquagesima. It has a new unknown name. A Cambridge undergraduate read the Epistle: I could not understand it. If he had read it in the old version it would have read, 'Though I speak with the tongues of men and of angels and have not charity, I am become as sounding brass, or a tinkling cymbal.' So what is he doing, silly young man, reading one of the greatest passages both of St. Paul and of English literature in a down-to-earth piece of bald prose? That is madness.

At the Holy Communion the priest is made to invite everyone to come to the sacrament and he is to invite them all firmly to resolve to live in peace and love with all men. What is he doing, this priest? We grew up in the age of Hitler. And in those days Christianity seemed to be the true moral foundation of Europe, against those ideals or counter-ideals that the Nazis put forward. Should we really resolve to be in love and peace with all men? It is hardly a Christian thing to resolve. The attitude represented in such a phrase is weak-kneed. We need to go back to the Old Testament, to find, if we can, an Amos; to look for an Amos or an Isaiah to come and talk to the whole people of this country. 'Is not my word like a fire, saith the Lord, and like a hammer that breaketh the rock into pieces?' There is some kind of failure of nerve going on which is a shutting up of the Church's message, talking up its own sleeve, prophesying into its own waistcoat pocket.

History teaches that disestablishments do not occur except in two circumstances. One is a racial difference between the Protestants against establishment and the established Church, as happened for example in Ireland in 1869 or Wales in 1914 or in Canada. And second is a revolution in the State which reconstructs all the institutions of the State and this is the way in which Churches were disestablished in our times in Germany, Spain, France and Central America. This applies only to a full and formal act of separation between Church and State. The Swedes argue at the moment whether or not they may in this decade totally separate Church from State; if they did, it would be a new thing because they would have neither the racial motives nor the revolutionary motives for the action which they contemplate taking, and it remains to be seen whether it will happen.

The whole force of British history is not in surgical operations but in steady evolution. We are the only country in the world which has not had a revolution since 1688 and that is a proud record, a great mark both of the stability of this country and of its willingness to adapt, little by little, bit by bit, to the necessities of new times.

The Church exists for humanity, and not for itself. It does not exist to prophesy into its own waistcoat pocket.

There has been discussion recently over the reform of the Second Chamber. The proposals of the late 1960s affect the position of bishops in the House of Lords. The Church and State Commission of 1970 recommended that leaders of other denominations, besides bishops of the Church of England, should have seats in the House of Lords; in such a reform there would not be so many bishops as now. It is not the case that if we retain any link between Queen and Church, which means a link between State and Church, we would necessarily have to retain all the existing arrangements of those links. I am speaking rather to the mainstream.

The State might at some point hold that as this country has become too plural, and as it now has religions of every sort, and as many of its people have no religion, it would be better that we free all the organs of the State from any relationship to any Church. If the State says that, then God bless the State. That is their affair and the Church should accept it with equanimity. But if the Church said it to the State then it is a refusal of a high vocation and a failure of nerve.

THE TWO KINGDOMS

Victor de Waal

4 The Two Kingdoms

by Victor de Waal

Every time I stand at the High Altar of Canterbury
Cathedral I stand in the presence of eighty-eight figures
surrounding me in the clerestory windows. They were
placed there by the monastic community in the
thirteenth century, and they were deliberately chosen to
underline the Old Testament descent of Christ, not
from the royal line of David but from the patriarchs,
priests and prophets that, in Luke's genealogy, stretch
back to Adam. In this the monks of Canterbury were
unlike their brothers in the royal abbey of St. Denis
across the water in France. At Canterbury they wanted
no emphasis on kingship and did not give the tree of
Jesse pride of place.

In the other windows too, around the shrine of St.
Thomas Becket, the scenes portray again and again the
Church's supremacy over temporal rulers: kings obey
the apostles Peter and Paul; the Emperor Constantine is
dissuaded by the Church from the slaughter of children
(two among many examples) – an emphasis on the
Church's authority to be expected from a monastic
foundation continually appealing to the Pope against the
King, a community that had had an Archbishop
martyred for his stand against the Crown. No wonder
one of Henry VIII's first moves in his bid to take control

of the Church of England was utterly to destroy Becket's shrine, though the despoilers did not dare to touch the windows that told his story, or perhaps they did not perceive their carefully planned, politically sophisticated message; and so they are there to this day – not, as is commonly thought, the pictorial bible of the poor, but an illustrated political statement.

Becket forced the Church of his day and of the following century to come to grips with the issue of temporal and spiritual power, an issue of such burning importance that devotion to the Canterbury martyr was immediately taken up throughout Europe as far afield as Sweden and Hungary, and it is still alive today. And today in Canterbury it seems entirely appropriate that by the site of his shrine there should be celebrated the martyrs of our own time, Dietrich Bonhoeffer of Nazi Germany, Archbishop Luwum of Uganda, Archbishop Oscar Romero of El Salvador, and other Christian leaders who stood out for conscience's sake against tyrannical rulers.

Thomas Becket posed a threat to the political establishment of his day, a threat still incipient and so powerful that three and a half centuries later the king felt the need to try to obliterate his memory (destroy his shrine, cutting his name from the calendar of saints, ordering it to be crossed out in the service books). He posed a threat because, as Lord Chancellor and Archbishop, Thomas Becket spoke from within the very heart of the establishment. His prophetic voice came not from some place outside the camp where it could be disregarded or ignored as irrelevant or eccentric. It spoke from within the middle of the circle, it made all those sitting in the places of power look at each other uncomfortably.

As we reflect on the subject of Church and State, it is this above all that I want to hold before you: that for the Church to speak with the voice of Christ it has to speak not from outside but from *within* the societies of men and women engaged in the affairs of the world. Only so can the prophetic word speak with the truth that actually enlightens and *changes* people's hearts and lives.

In England today we are bound to reflect on the lives of three such prophets who, in separate and individual ways, took a stand on the issue of Church and State. They have little in common, except this one feature: they were all members of the establishment. One was an MP, another an Oxford don, the third a bishop of the Church of England.

William Wilberforce, who died three days after the completion of his life's work, when on July 26th, 1833 Parliament finally abolished slavery, was a prosperous, middle-class businessman, the MP for Hull.

John Keble, poet and theologian, an academic don in conservative Oxford, preached in the University church on July 14th, 1833 the assize sermon on 'National Apostasy' that began the Oxford Movement.

George Bell, a patron of the arts, a tireless worker for Christian unity, Dean of Canterbury and then Bishop of Chichester with a traditional seat in the House of Lords, and a lonely critic of Britain's war policy, was born exactly 100 years ago on February 4th, 1883.

With hindsight the question of slavery and the slave-trade seems to us so clear-cut a moral issue that it is astonishing that Christians tolerated it for so long, and that as recently as a century and a half ago the arguments for and against abolition posed a genuine moral dilemma for sincere Christians.

But slaves were private property, and it was deeply felt that any encroachment on the right of private property was a threat to individual liberty, a vital value not only in the political sphere, but for Christianity itself. The paradox that the possession of slaves was necessary to Christian liberty was an irony, an absurdity, far from being immediately apparent to our quite recent forebears. Even if slavery was admitted by many to be itself abhorrent, it was better, so it was genuinely argued, to tolerate it for the greater good of maintaining a property-owning civilised society. The abolition of slavery would lead inexorably to the excesses and chaos of the French Revolution; it would make for the disintegration of the Christianly ordered world.

This was a powerful argument at the time, espoused by devout Christians, and if it seems strange to us now, it is well to realise that its reasoning is paralleled today, for example, among those who believe that the evermore costly development and threatened first use of nuclear weapons (though abhorrent in themselves) are justified by the greater perceived evil that they are meant to avoid. That reasoning is paralleled whenever we fail to realise that evil means cannot lead to a morally good end, that the only godly way to *achieve* good is to *do* good. At the heart of the Gospel is the insight that the only risks worth taking as human beings are the risks of love.

William Wilberforce used his position as an MP to make the House of Commons the arena for his struggle, and he and his friends made use of all the media of their time – the press, the organising of petitions, the making of campaign buttons – to further their cause. (Josiah Wedgwood's pottery medallions, the forerunners of lapel buttons, became immensely popular and appeared even on snuffboxes and hairpins. They showed a kneeling black manacled figure with the legend, 'Am not I a man and a brother?')

John Keble was equally realistic in the academic establishment of the university world. He and his friends, a band of prophets, preached sermons and printed and published the *Tracts for the Times*. They challenged the right of Parliament to legislate for the Church and sought to arouse a decadent Church of England to become again aware of itself. The issue which he termed 'national apostasy' concerned the suppression of seemingly redundant Irish bishoprics, an issue that, unlike Wilberforce's crusade, seems as peripheral to us as Becket's defence of the clergy's right to be tried only in ecclesiastical courts. But it takes a prophet's insight to see the larger issue that is at stake in an apparently small step, to perceive (as if by looking into the future) what long-term consequences would follow from an apparently trivial compromise of moral principle.

Thus to take a modern example, few Germans, citizens of one of the most culturally respected civilised nations of Europe, perceived in 1933 what would be the implications of voting for Adolf Hitler. They admitted that some of his policies, especially his fervent anti-Semitism, were extreme. But they felt that no doubt these could be excused in the light of the general good he promised to bring Germany. Would they have voted for him if they could have forseen Auschwitz and Belsen as the inexorable consequences of his programme? Probably not, yet most German Christians supported him and only a minority (numbering, for example, Dietrich Bonhoeffer among them) were prepared to form themselves in due course into an opposition 'Confessing Church'.

The issue confronting German Christians in the 1930s may be compared to the flaring up of a long smouldering illness into a sudden and terrible crisis, a crisis which when it is overcome leaves the patient altogether cured. The sickness I refer to is the rise of European nationalism in the Middle Ages and the subordinating of the Church's authority to the secular power of the State. This became strongest in countries influenced by the Lutheran Reformation, such as Germany, and is true also of England. Already in the fourteenth century the political theorist Marsilius of Padua had proposed the overturning of priestly hegemony, the authority of the spiritual power over the temporal, claimed by papal apologists in the medieval West.

For Luther the laity ruled, and also ruled the Church as a human social institution, leaving to the clergy only their rights in 'spiritual' matters. Does that sound familiar? Do we not hear it in England again and again in protests that the Church should keep out of politics and confine itself to saving souls? England, like Germany, was deeply infected by this doctrine, of which the cry 'no popery' became the slogan. That infection in England has not come up to the monstrous crisis that it reached in Germany before the war, when Christians had to choose between what they perceived to be their Christian conscious loyalty to the temporal ruler set over them by God, even if he were Hitler, and a rebellion motivated by Christian convictions alien to their centuries-long doctrine of a Church subservient to the State. Most, as we know, chose the former course, some even backing Hitler's worst excesses.

In England the struggle of conscience has been altogether less dramatic. Parliament's rejection of the 1928 Prayer Book was perhaps its highest point. But it has grumbled away ever since Keble's assize sermon, as the Church of England wrests piecemeal from a reluctant Crown and Parliament the right to conduct its own affairs. And even as it does so the Church of England seems, in a way difficult entirely to grasp or analyse, to continue to engage the nation's attention.

Consider how the Synod debate on 'the Church and the Bomb', and its outcome, was clearly a concern for the government and the media, while the similar debate last May in the General Assembly of the Church of Scotland hardly raised a ripple. Did you know even, that the Church of Scotland, the other highly respectable established Church in these islands, then actually decided to condemn the possession by this country of nuclear weapons as inconsistent with the teachings of Christ?

The reason is that the Church's establishment in Scotland, as in other countries like Holland, whose

Christianity was deeply influenced by Calvin and not by Luther, is based on a quite other conception of the relation of Church and State than that taught by that so influential Marsilius of Padua long ago in the fourteenth century. The establishment of the Church of Scotland has always been one in which, unlike England, not only the individual Christian but the Church as an institution has been independent of the temporal ruler. And this has allowed the Church an inner freedom corporately to come to grips with the moral dimensions of the world's political concerns in a way which may be heeded or not by the State, but is not necessarily felt by that State to threaten its own rights.

We can see therefore that the question of the Church's establishment or disestablishment is not as simple as might at first appear. Establishment can mean ecclesiastical supremacy over all affairs of State; it can mean the incorporation of the Church into one political system under a godly or ungodly prince (a view that underlies, for example, the 'Prayer for the whole state of Christ's Church' in the Prayer Book); it can mean, as in Scotland, a profound cultural link which yet preserves institutional independence.

A year ago I doubt whether the issue of Church and State (and of the merits of establishment and dis-establishment) would have been raised. What seems to have happened is that suddenly in England, as has been the case for a generation in other parts of the world (for example, in some countries of Eastern Europe, in South Africa, in Central and South America, in the Philippines), the qualifications of those in political power to make judgments (in effect moral judgments) about wealth, about human rights (I am thinking of immigrants), and about war and peace have been challenged; and challenged for the first time by the institutional Church, or by what are perceived to be influential sections within it. And curiously the reaction of those in political power has *not* been to accelerate the long creeping process of disestablishment, pushing the Church even more to those fringes of society to which many had thought it had long ago been relegated. The reaction has been rather an attempt, even by the Prime Minister and the government, by Members of Parliament, by the right-wing media, to reassert control over the Church.

And interestingly this is a reaction parallel to that seen in the other parts of the world I have mentioned. For few states, whatever they may profess (even Marxist states), are truly secular. Every empire, every nation, has within it a tendency to claim for itself something supernatural. And that has always meant that it has been uncomfortable with a Church that has supernatural claims of its own. It will fight the Church, or it will try to take it over: what it finds most difficult is to tolerate it. The Roman Empire moved in the space of fifty years, in the fourth century, from persecuting Christianity to a brief period of toleration, then to making it compulsory. No Christian was allowed in the army (nor wanted to be); a generation later *only* Christians were allowed in!

The quasi-supernatural claims of the State take an extreme form in totalitarian regimes which claim to order not only the external lives but the interior dispositions, thoughts and beliefs of their citizens. In East Germany it is all but impossible for a professing Christian to gain admittance to higher education. If we think that is intolerant, it is well to remember that not much more than a century ago it was impossible to gain admittance to Oxford or Cambridge, even if one was a Christian, unless one could subscribe to the 39 Articles of the Church of England!

It is Christians in Eastern Europe who, adopting Marxist terminology, have come to designate their position vis-à-vis the State as 'critical solidarity'. And I would like to suggest to you that this phrase could enshrine for us the attitude most appropriate for the relation between Christians and the society to which we belong, between Church and State today.

The temptation of the Church is to wash its hands of the world, to tell it some home truths, and then to opt out into some private 'spiritual' sphere. That would be easier for the Church, and much easier for those it addresses, who can then write it off as irrelevant to the concerns that must be the province of politicians, economists, and social engineers. Much more disturbing, much more dangerous to the established order is a Church which never gives up its solidarity with its contemporaries, never gives up its membership in society. And much more difficult for the Church itself. And this solidarity is the only possible legitimate base for prophecy. Jeremiah could easily have left Jerusalem when he foresaw its inevitable doom, but he stayed with it to the end, though attacked and persecuted for his warnings. In the same way Jesus, and St. Paul after him, taught a basic loyalty to the authority of the State, however hostile to their message, an authority limited only by the refusal to grant Caesar the tribute due only to God.

There is no opting out of the concerns, the problems and the responsibilities of those among whom we live. Christianity (as the anonymous author of the Epistle to Diognetus wrote in the second century AD) is not living a special or separate kind of life from that of the ordinary world but points to the way an ordinary life in the world should and can be lived by individual persons, by social groups, by nations themselves as human entities. And that means that the Church in all its members has to stay and concern itself with all the social, economic and political issues of society. But its solidarity is 'critical' because, while identifying with the overall aims and purposes of the country in which it lives, it submits these aims and purposes to the critical appraisal that stems from its own moral tradition about what human beings are meant to be, a tradition stretching back to the Bible and transcending national boundaries. In the words of the New Testament, it owes allegiance also to another king as well as to Caesar.

The third person whose anniversary falls this year, George Bell, sometime Dean of Canterbury and then Bishop of Chichester, summed up in his person in a way unique in this century in England this prophetic quality of 'critical solidarity'.

As an Englishman and a churchman he entered deeply into the culture of this country and found the means to bring to life much that was dormant in our tradition. The Cathedral at Canterbury under his guidance blossomed into a renewed life which, sixty years later, still inspires its worship, its pilgrimage, and above all its concern with the living arts, a revival that has spread throughout the English Church and, indeed, widely into the life of other Churches. In Chichester also his patronage brought modern painters and sculptors into the service of the Church.

But just as the arts themselves transcend national boundaries, so Bell perceived that the Church itself can find its truest life, its catholicity, only if it is rooted both in the culture of its own country and also transcends that culture in unity with Christians of other cultures and nations. His commitment to the arts and his ecumenism are of a piece. His work for the founding of the World Council of Churches is of a piece with his work for understanding and reconciliation between the nationalisms of the Europe of his day, soon taken to the extremes of war. And during that war he continued to argue for negotiation between the Allies and the opponents of Hitler in Germany, seeing in the policy of 'unconditional surrender' and the bombing of the civilian populations of German cities a betrayal of fundamental Christian principle. His 'critical solidarity' with his own country at war was of a piece with his support in the 1930s of those Christians who in

Germany were led to oppose Hitler. He wrote, he spoke in the House of Lords, he was deeply unpopular, he was disregarded, and he was passed over when by right of his outstanding stature he should have become Archbishop of Canterbury.

But to many Christians today, not only in England, his clarity of prophetic vision is an inspiration in times that may become even darker than his own, and his mode of 'critical solidarity' remains a model of that relation of Church and State, which only is true to the Church's nature, and which only is healthy for the State itself.

Our country is not a totalitarian one, and Christians with many others have to be deeply thankful for the freedoms of speech, of writing and of association which we enjoy. But it would be surprising if in our own nation too there were not those who find in the Church's prophetic stances, its 'critical solidarity', a threat which they fear, and to which they react with hostility when they perceive the Church expressing political views about the conduct of the nation which are in conflict with their own. As the issue of riches and poverty, at home and overseas, becomes more and more clear-cut (as it must), so that conflict will increase. And that conflict will be for the Church in this country, as it is in other nations, all the more painful in that Christians are bound to be divided among themselves in what they see and recognise.

For myself I believe that we cannot delay much longer, as individual Christians and as a Church, in making up our minds about the two great moral issues of our time – the fair sharing of the resources of our planet, and the refusal to let fear rule our lives – and in working out and living by the consequences. of our decision. For the Church's prophetic voice to be heard, it must come from Christians like William Wilberforce, like John Keble, like George Bell, profoundly engaged in the affairs of the world.

Only so will it be heard to be speaking true, whether to

be obeyed or rejected. Only so will it be the voice of Christ speaking with authority to change people's hearts and lives. Only so will they be able to make up their minds to which king they owe their fundamental allegiance.

A CASE FOR THE DISESTABLISHMENT OF THE CHURCH OF ENGLAND

Tony Benn

5 A Case for the Disestablishment of
the Church of England

by Tony Benn

I would like to take this opportunity to argue the case for the liberation of the Anglican Church from the British State by the disestablishment of the Church of England.

Though I was confirmed as an Anglican I have, over the years, become more and more interested in the relevance of the social message of Jesus, the carpenter of Nazareth, about peace, justice and the brotherhood and sisterhood of all humanity, from which so much of the Socialist faith derives, and less and less concerned with matters of doctrine, mystery and mythology, though I deeply respect those whose beliefs centre on the creeds.

I was brought up to believe in 'the priesthood of all believers' and retain considerable scepticism about those bishops and clergy who might claim a prescriptive right to interpose their own interpretation of the gospels, or the faith, between the people and the Creator – still more if those same bishops have been appointed by political patronage.

In short, I regard myself as a serious student of the teachings of Jesus – no more and no less.

My argument is a simple one and can be briefly summarised. It is that the teachings of Jesus, about brotherhood and sisterhood and peace, and the need to preach them freely, have acquired a new urgency and importance in the crisis which now threatens to overwhelm the world, and must necessarily lead many Christians to challenge the role of the State as the instrument of government, and the status quo which it sustains, and hence should not be subject to State power.

Similarly, governments which are elected by people of all denominations and none, to represent them all, cannot any longer legitimately maintain one denomination or faith in a privileged position in relation to those who are members of other religions, other denominations, or who are atheists, agnostics or humanists.

The debate about the establishment of the Church of England goes far back into our history, and has, in the past, aroused great passions. As recently as 1970 the Chadwick Commission on 'Church and State' dealt with this very issue.

Britain has a tradition of Christianity dating back many centuries and the Synod of Whitby in 664 recognised the Pope as the head of the Church in England, with powers over its organisation and theology. He also had discretion in the appointment of archbishops and bishops, and supervision over the work and discipline of the Church – with considerable powers over taxation. Indeed, in 1376 a petition to the House of Commons protested that the taxes paid to the Pope 'amounts to five times the tax from all the King's annual benefits from the whole kingdom'.

Canon Law was made in Rome and modified to meet local customs. Moreover, the King depended upon the Church to provide financial, diplomatic and administrative talent. In that sense, the Church was established even during those centuries before the Reformation and the break with Rome; because it was the religion of the Crown, and successive monarchs upheld the authority of the Church and, in turn, had their authority upheld by the Church.

Spiritual and temporal powers sustained each other by a complicated system of mutual allegiance and support. Pope Gregory VII (1073 to 1085) stated plainly that 'The Pope is the master of Emperors'. Charlemagne, in a letter to Pope Leo III, asked the Holy Father to 'help our armies' so that 'Christian people may everywhere and always have the victory over the enemies of His Holy Name.' King John of England was forced by a papal interdict and his own excommunication in 1209 to surrender the kingdom to Pope Innocent III, receiving it back as a fiefdom in 1213.

The Crown accepted papal supremacy because it embodied the doctrine that the King derived his legitimacy and authority by 'divine right', which the Church then defended against republicans, democrats, pretenders to the throne and other troublemakers. The survival of the Coronation as a quasi-sacrament is a reminder of that principle. It was equally convenient for the Pope, who required the submission of the King in matters of faith and relied upon the King to protect the Church against heresy, schism, apostasy and other troubles. Thus was Henry VIII recognised as a Defender of the Faith for his denunciation of Martin Luther in 1521, a title retained by successive monarchs to this day, centuries after the break with Rome, of which we are reminded with the abbreviated words FID DEF (or just F D) on our coins.

Nor should it be thought that this medieval version of the position of the Crown has vanished from the teachings of some clergy. A few weeks ago I visited Canewdon parish church in Essex and the vicar, the Rev. Norman Kelly, gave me his parish letter dated November 1982, in which he had written: 'The Monarch, the Queen, is the Law, and no one else . . . Why cannot the Queen do wrong and be prosecuted like us? Because the Monarch is the source of law, just as God cannot sin, because God is the source of goodness.'

*

The conflict which developed between the Pope and Henry VIII culminated in a complete break and the Acts of Supremacy of 1534, and those that followed it, required all subjects to recognise the Crown as head of the new Church of England, and to accept that Church as the only legitimate Church. This was a political and not a theological breach. It protected the State from criticism by the Church, thus creating the very problem which now strengthens the State and weakens the Church.

The real issue hinged on who should exercise ecclesiastical power in England, and the controversy over the King's marriage to Anne Boleyn in 1533, which the Pope would not allow, was the occasion rather than the cause of the dispute. But what emerged was a nationalised Church, suppressing others, first subject to the King's personal authority; and then, as the powers of the Crown came, over the centuries, to be shared with Parliament and people, the control of the Church passed with it.

Theological arguments ebbed and flowed within the Church, and Parliament insisted upon conformity with its decisions. The Blasphemy Act of 1697, which made it a criminal offence for Christians to 'deny any one of the persons in the Holy Trinity to be God', was only repealed in 1967. The Bible, long kept out of the hands of the laity for fear that it might undermine the authority of the priests, and encourage those who were campaigning for social justice, could only be printed by the authority of the King, as it had first been by Henry VIII. The Book of Common Prayer was a schedule to the 1662 Act of Uniformity and the original text, in the Houses of Parliament, still carries the jagged ribbons by which it was attached to that Act. These successive acts of uniformity were strictly enforced against all dissenters and independents.

The Royal prerogative by which archbishops, bishops, deans and others were appointed was transferred to the de facto control of successive prime ministers who still today are free to exercise their discretion as between candidates recommended by the Church's Crown Appointments Commission, as Mrs Thatcher did in appointing Bishop Leonard to the diocese of London in 1981, though it is believed he was not the first choice of the Church.

The two archbishops and the bishops of London, Durham and Winchester automatically sit in the House of Lords along with others who enter, in rotation by seniority, all exercising, as Lords Spiritual, their rights to speak and vote as legislators. At the same time Anglican priests are held to be disqualified from election to the House of Commons on the grounds that they are represented by their bishops in the House of Lords – a disqualification criticised by the Bishop of Bath and Wells in his 1982 Christmas message. The argument for this disqualification is not sustainable since the appointment of bishops precludes a democratic election from that clerical 'representation'.

In addition, the Church has its own Assembly for handling its own internal affairs, which was made possible by the Enabling Act.

In practice, the Church of England has become a residual and comprehensive spiritual home for all who wish to use its services in the parishes in which they live, providing official support for the role of religion under the Crown as part of the social fabric of our society, now tolerant of all religions. Opposition to disestablishment would come from those who accept this system and fear that if its continuity was disturbed it might destabilise and secularise our whole way of life and diminish the influence of religion in all its manifestations.

However, other denominations have, over the centuries, suffered varying degrees of discrimination and oppression.

Roman Catholics were often persecuted. Since 1689 no Catholic has been allowed to ascend the Throne or marry the Monarch, and the Catholic Emancipation Act, allowing the Catholic hierarchy to return to England, was not passed until 1829. Even today Catholics are not allowed to appoint a primate, nor are Catholic priests allowed to stand for Parliament.

Nonconformists were equally harassed, as by the Five Mile Act of 1665, which prohibited independents from preaching within five miles of any corporate town.

It was not until 1871 that Catholics and Nonconformists were even allowed to attend Oxford or Cambridge universities.

The Jews were driven from England by an edict of Richard I in 1290 and they were not allowed back into Britain until 1656, in Cromwell's time, when the Lord Protector was influenced to readmit them by theological arguments advanced by a rabbi from Amsterdam. Jews were disqualified from sitting in Parliament until 1858. Disraeli was baptised as a Christian and no practising Jew has ever been Prime Minister.

Even today Catholics and Jews, and those practising other faiths or none, are still, in a sense, second-class theological citizens in that they cannot look to the State, as of right, to protect their faith, even though their rituals, schools and customs may be respected and protected by Parliament.

We have grown so accustomed to these arrangements that their manifest absurdities and dangers are hardly noticed and rarely discussed in public.

How, for example, can we justify a situation where the Monarch combines the functions of being, at one and the same time, supreme governor of the Church of England when in England, but who changes her denomination to preside over the Church of Scotland when in Scotland –

even though in that capacity she enjoys no power of patronage nor can Parliament intervene in Scottish Church affairs.

Is it not strange that the Church of England, which still will not allow the ordination of women to the priesthood, should accept a woman as its supreme governor, albeit with powers that do not extend into spiritual matters?

How can a Church preserve its spiritual integrity when its Prayer Book may still, in theory, be amended, or a new one rejected, as in 1928, by a parliament composed of members who are not required to be Anglicans or even Christians? Even the devolution of the powers to the Church in the 1974 Church of England (Worship and Doctrine) Measure, passed by Parliament is, in constitutional theory, capable of repeal by Parliament restoring Parliament's direct control over these matters. How can the Church accept a situation in which its archbishops and bishops are appointed by a Prime Minister who could be a Catholic, a Jew, a Congregationalist, a Humanist, a Muslim or a Hindu?

Suppose for a moment that the Church of England was not now established and imagine the public outcry there would be if a Member of Parliament were to demand the nationalisation of that Church to subject its leaders to political patronage and control of the order of its services. Or suppose it was argued that State control should now be extended to cover the Catholic, Nonconformist, Jewish, Buddhist, Hindu or Muslim communities.

These are all powerful arguments for disestablishment, but the case is stronger still if we examine the actual effects of having an established Church in the current situation.

Take first the attitude of Christians to the issue of nuclear war. Many Christians who are not pacifists have now concluded that the old doctrine of a just war cannot apply to the production, ownership or use of nuclear weapons which would escalate armed conflict to the levels of genocide.

The Bishop of Salisbury, who chaired the Committee which wrote the report *The Church and the Bomb*, has raised this very issue and has won wide public support for its conclusions even though it was rejected by the Synod. In 1982 the Assembly of the Church of Scotland voted by 255 votes to 143 in favour of unilateral nuclear disarmament.

But could the established Church of England take up a position on nuclear weapons that brought it into direct conflict with the government, while the Crown remained the titular head of both Church and State? Mr Peter Blaker, the Minister of State for Defence, made this point on ITN on August 6th 1982, when he said: 'Obviously we would not be happy if the Church of England was to adopt a policy different from that of the Government.'

In America, where the Catholic bishops and other Church leaders have warned against the dangers of nuclear war, no such constitutional problem can arise, since the separation of Church and State is a foundation stone of the American constitution. Such pressure as is brought on American Church leaders has to be informal.

Even the mild and reasonable arguments for the spirit of reconciliation, which the Archbishop of Canterbury introduced into his sermon at the Service of Thanksgiving at St Paul's Cathedral after the Falklands War, apparently incurred the displeasure of the Prime Minister, who seems to have wanted a more militaristic celebration of the victory. And why not, since she appoints both archbishops and bishops?

Given that power of patronage, what bishop or cleric, with hopes of moving into Lambeth Palace or Bishopthorpe, would now dare to mount a sustained campaign against the militarism and jingoism which are officially blessed from No. 10 Downing Street? Some courageous churchmen, like the late Archbishop Temple, did speak out and won preferment, but not everyone is possessed of that sort of character. We shall see when the new Archbishop of York is appointed whether the political preferences of the Prime Minister are decisive.

Establishment necessarily involves a subtle corruption of the spirit of the Church, because it is safely embedded in the wider establishment of society, which includes the privileged and the powerful. The strong cannot credibly preach the gospels to the weak. That, in essence, is what those who preach Liberation Theology in Latin America are saying.

How can those Christians who see monetarism being so cruelly applied to the old, the sick, the homeless, women, the black community and the young unemployed, lead a struggle against this injustice from within an established Church subject to a Cabinet and a parliamentary majority composed of those very people who are responsible for implementing those very policies?

These problems also extend to theological matters. The Pope's visit to Britain in 1982 and his historic meeting with Dr Runcie in Canterbury Cathedral opened up new prospects of Christian unity. And if anyone doubts the desire of some Anglicans for some such union, it may be inferred from the defeat by the Synod of the covenant which would have brought the Church of England and the Free Churches together, but at the expense, so it was feared by some, of the prospects of full reunion with Rome. Other reasons which may have played a part in the defeat of the covenant were the problem of the episcopacy and the ordination of women, which has been accepted in some Free Churches but which the Church of Rome has consistently rejected despite some support for it amongst the Catholic laity.

But even if all these problems could be resolved, a

nationalised Church could never take its proper place in the world ecumenical movement. Yet the teachings of Jesus have spread across the world and know no national boundaries. Like the ideas of Socialism, they are international in outlook and perspective. That is another powerful reason for liberating the Church from the control of any nation state with its national, rather than its international, outlook. Religious conviction is also a very personal act and cannot be regimented by legislation or enforced by the State. So, both the international nature of Christianity and its reflection in personal faith, point away from the idea of having a State religion.

I believe that the time has come to begin a national campaign for disestablishment. How it is to be done can be safely left for future discussion. It would certainly end all ministerial and parliamentary control over appointments, doctrine and worship, and end the automatic right of bishops to sit in the House of Lords. It would necessarily free the Monarch of the day to worship in any way that he or she might wish, or not at all, as a member of any Church or none.

The financial arrangements would need to be looked at separately, and if Parliament thought it right that any public money should be paid to the Church of England, for example for the upkeep of cathedrals or church buildings, the financial claims of other denominations would need to be considered on the basis of absolute equality.

All this could be settled once the principle of disestablishment had been agreed. There are of course clear precedents to guide us. The Church in Wales was disestablished in 1920 after the passage of the 1914 Welsh Church Act. Since then the Crown has not had the power to appoint bishops in Wales and such bishops do not sit in the House of Lords, and no significant body of opinion has been expressed in favour of re-establishing it as a State Church.

There is certainly support within the Church of England for disestablishment and many in the Anglican community worldwide might welcome and approve the liberation of the Church of England to release it to work more effectively. Disestablishment might also appeal to the large Catholic community, to the Free Churches and even to the Church of Scotland, which is in a special position, established but not under direct State control. In addition, there are over a million Jews, Buddhists, Hindus, Muslims and Sikhs and, according to the Gallup polls, over a quarter of the whole population would classify themselves as Humanists, following no particular faith, who might favour a change that gave them equality of status.

The case for disestablishment thus rests on various grounds: historical and theological; practical and moral; constitutional and democratic; international and equitable. But the strongest case of all, as it would need to be argued within the Anglican community, would necessarily hinge on the argument for liberation. As the crisis of our society deepens, the moral basis that must underpin all political judgments is becoming clearer and clearer, and the Church must be liberated from its subservience to the State.

Britain needs a liberation theology which has the courage to preach against the corruption of power by speaking for those who are its victims. Nowhere is that more necessary than in the inner cities where the poverty and deprivation are most acute, and where hard-pressed Anglican clergy feel themselves under the greatest pressure compared to their colleagues with more prosperous suburban or rural parishes. The Church needs freedom, to challenge the decisions of government, of Parliament and the whole establishment, and the materialist values which have elevated the worship of money above all else – and the people need to know that these rotten values are not endorsed by a State religion.

If democracy is to reflect through its decisions the deeper needs of humanity, and its aspirations for international peace and justice, and for brotherhood and sisterhood in our relations with each other, we must now break the link between Church and State.

Politics and the Church

Teddy Taylor

6 Politics and the Church

by Teddy Taylor

The recent agitated discussions within the Church of England about nuclear weapons have been regarded by some commentators as being a relatively new phenomenon, but the issue of whether the Church should give a lead or express a view on political issues is one which has perplexed and divided the Church from its earliest days.

Throughout history there have been groups, denominations and individuals who have argued that the Christian Church should have no involvement in political issues whatsoever. Other groups and denominations have argued that Christian people and the Church have a duty to consider together the practical issues facing men and women in their everyday lives and to spell out policies and answers to problems in the light of the teachings of Jesus Christ.

It is recorded, for example, that when the practice of Christianity was made lawful under Emperor Constantine, people in leading positions in the army and administration worked together and no doubt prayed together to establish what we might loosely call Christian policies. But it is also recorded that St. Anthony considered that the involvement of Christian people in political decisions diverted them from the teachings of Christ and he led his followers into the Egyptian desert to separate them from the corruption of civic and public life.

When Oliver Cromwell got down to the business of managing England's affairs, one of his many experiments in democracy was to establish a so-called 'Assembly of Saints' on the basis that Christian leaders following Christian principles could arrive at better decisions than the normal run of party politicians.

A recent splendid paperback book on the life of John Calvin relates in detail how a 'saintly city' was established in Geneva in which Calvin's Christian followers not only tried to give him a lead but actually took over the entire political system and the courts on the basis that decisions and judgments made by Christians should lead to a better and more godly pattern of living. And it is recorded that individuals were sentenced severely by the Church courts for such crimes as 'dancing', for 'claiming that the Pope was a good man' and 'for alleging that the influx of Huguenot immigrants had led to an increase in the cost of living.'

At other times in history, leaders of the Church issued advice or instructions to political leaders to persecute sects and denominations which were believed to be promoting incorrect interpretations of the Gospel. And today in Britain we have a sharp divide between those who argue that the Church is utterly irrelevant if it cannot provide at least guidance and leadership on key political issues, and those who argue that for the Church to be involved in politics deflects individuals from the Christian message.

In Central and South America the issue is topical and vital, with the Pope urging his priests not to be involved in political leadership while, in the same nations, there are priests and other clergymen who consider that it would be a denial of all that Christ preached if they were to do nothing to oppose regimes which deny freedom and liberty and engage in foul repression.

So the problems of the Church of England Synod are not unique. But there is a difference in the range of debate by comparison with countries like those in Central America. Few people in the British Churches would seek to argue that the Church should give a lead in opposing the system of government in Britain. Few would argue that the Church should advise its members to give or deny support to particular political parties. But there is a strong body of opinion that the Church should have clear policies and give a clear lead on broad issues like, for example, nuclear weapons, apartheid, immigration, unemployment and welfare.

It is in this narrower field that the debate is taking place in the UK and it is in this area that Christians should be exercising their judgments. My view is clear. I believe that, while individual Christians have a duty to play an active part in politics as one of the vehicles of showing concern for their fellow men, it is pointless and contrary to the teachings of scripture for the Church, for those holding leadership within the Church and for organisations within the Church to seek to arrive at so-called 'Christian policies' to deal with political problems.

There are three basic reasons why I hold this view. First, I find it difficult to see any political issue in terms of absolute right and absolute wrong – and even if it were possible to find such an issue, I cannot believe that the Almighty would make an equal judgment of the multitude of motives which led individuals to support one particular view.

On the complexity of issues, we need look no further than the issues of war and of nuclear weapons. There were Christian pacifists, for example, who opposed our entering the Second World War because of their objection to killing under any circumstances. But if we had not entered that war, would not the Christian pacifists have carried some responsibility for killing if, because of our inaction, 300,000 British Jews had been sent to gas chambers.

In the same way, some argue that if we abandoned nuclear weapons then at least we would be personally freed from the guilt of mass killing if such weapons ever came to be used. I've just returned from a trip to North-West Pakistan, where I visited the pathetic refugee camps in which about one third of the whole population of Afghanistan have settled following the Russian invasion. There has been an appalling blood-bath in Afghanistan and I saw many of the victims. Is it not possible that the killings could have been avoided if the non-aligned Afghanistan had been in a collective defence agreement with somebody's nuclear umbrella as part of it?

It's the same for MPs when it comes to capital punishment. There are many arguments for and against it, but if our judgment leads us to the conclusion that lives would be saved if capital punishment were restored, would we not carry some responsibility for any such loss of life by voting for abolition?

On each of these issues there are sharply conflicting views, but I would challenge anyone to deny that people could take different views for caring and Christian reasons.

Second, if there is Church involvement in politics, we inevitably see the development of political Churches. To a small extent it is happening in the UK. When I came down to Southend from Scotland, and thereby lost my contact with the Church of Scotland, I was advised by a local Southender that I might be well advised to avoid joining one particular Nonconformist denomination because of what my adviser regarded as the political opinions which that denomination was linked with. I am told, although I do not know, that in South Africa supporters of apartheid tend to go to the Dutch Reformed Church, opponents tend to go to the Anglican Church and those who are not quite sure feel happy in the Presbyterian Church. Nothing, in my view, can tend to deflect people away from the teachings of the Gospel than to have Churches linked – perhaps only through imagery – with particular political beliefs.

But it is from the Gospel that Christians should take their guidance. If we ignore the messages of scripture, it is difficult to claim a Christian base for the view which we hold. The consistent message in the Gospels is that Christ, although constantly pressurised and challenged to express views on the political issues of the day, went out of His way to avoid any such determination.

Israel at that time was ruled by an illegal colonial regime. There was a multitude of political terrorists or freedom fighters in the hills anxious to cut Roman throats. There was clear discrimination in favour of Roman citizens, as we heard from St. Paul, which was more open to charges of racialism than any British nationality acts. It was in this setting that Christ was asked directly if it was lawful to pay taxes to this illegal colonial regime. And every Christian knows the answer which He gave.

Perhaps even more telling as an example was His response to those who thrust the adulterous woman before Him. There was, as you will recall, no doubt about the circumstances – she had been caught in the very act. There was no doubt about the legal penalty. The challenge was clear – and a 'Yes or No' answer seemed to be the only possibility. But what emerged from this was that it was the *motives* of the accusers which concerned Christ.

This, I believe, is the key to the Christian concept of politics. What should concern Christians is that, with the intelligence, knowledge and experience they have, they should approach the great political issues of the day with the motives which stem from following the teachings of Christ.

I can think of many current political issues which people approach with different motives. Some oppose nuclear weapons because they are deeply concerned for the welfare of their neighbours. Others oppose them because they believe that the destruction or under-mining of an undefended West will lead to the destruction of capitalism. Some support immigration controls because they are concerned that extra immi-gration will lead to a worsening of race relations; some support the same policy because they are instinctively suspicious towards people who look different; and some support them as a means of securing the votes of prejudiced people. I cannot believe that the Almighty would regard all these people in the same way because they supported the same policy.

I believe that some of the pressure to involve the Church in politics stems from a view that the absence of such involvement has led to empty churches and the alienation of the people from religion. The Church, it seems, has become unfashionable and unpopular. If this concerns you we should look at the account of Christ's life in the Gospels. There certainly isn't much evidence of popularity or of fashionable opinions. At the time, the people of Israel were desperate for leadership. Some sought a leader to free them from the tyranny of the Romans. Some sought a leader to restore the standing of the Jewish faith. Some sought a person to conduct a great moral crusade. But they were all disappointed.

There are many references in the Gospel to people at that time being amazed at Christ's teachings, of being astonished, of being perplexed and of being confused. But the only two instances of popularity were when He made a great speech condemning the Pharisees when the people 'heard Him gladly' and when He rode into Jerusalem on a donkey which was interpreted by some as an anti-authoritarian gesture.

And when He was nailed on the Cross, there were no civil demonstrations, no student riots, no stoning of Roman soldiers. Only a huddling together of a handful of shattered and terrified followers with one even denying knowledge of Christ.

The message which Christ taught is unique in that it is

relevant and vital at all times and in all circumstances. It is that message which should be preached and it must not be cheapened or diluted by seeking to link it with specific answers to the problems of the day. Just as Christ, in His only violent gesture, turned over the money-changers' tables because their activities and presence were polluting the temple, so I believe that Christ would turn with anger against those who seek to transform His mighty Church into a holy supporters' club for either the ladies at Greenham Common or for the Primrose League.

IN THE GLOBAL VILLAGE

Eric James

7 In the Global Village

by Eric James

When I was invited to speak in this series on 'Church and State', I agreed to speak on 'Church and State in a Global Village'. That title, when it reached the railings and other characteristic forms of St. James publicity, had become 'Church and State: A Global View' – which seems to credit me with a view somewhat above my station. Yet I am willing to stay with the general point that either title makes: that these days it is impossible for the Church to accept a relationship to the State which does not take into consideration the shape of the world. And the world today is shaped primarily – I have no doubt – by one factor above all others: the population explosion.

It helps me to get into perspective the 'Constantinian Settlement', if ever there was one, and the Elizabethan Settlement – and the latest form of it that the Church of England now enjoys in the reign of Elizabeth II – if I meditate a little on what I will call 'the time factor in relation to the world's population'.

It was, let us say, about 15,000 million years ago that our universe came to be; and 5,000 million years ago that life came to be; then came vertebrates; then reptiles; then mammals; then, less than 10 million years ago, came the anthropoids – animals almost like ourselves;

and in the very last second of the last hour of the one day
that forms the whole lifespan of the universe, Man came
to be; and several million years later we beheld on this
earth 'the Man', Jesus. And that is the event which gives
the possibility of there being a Church to relate to the
State.

When that central fact of our faith occurred: when
'the Word was made flesh and dwelt amongst us', there
were only about 250 million people in the world. A
thousand years later the family of man had grown to 350
million. It took, however, till about 1830 to reach the
world's first thousand million; but it took only 100 years
more to reach its second thousand million; and only
another thirty years to reach its third; and only another
fifteen years to reach its fourth, in 1975. And now, every
seven years, another 1000 million – another billion – is
added to the population of the world. And by 2000 AD
there will be 6000 million people in the world.

Now it is not the simple fact of population increase
that causes the present predicament of mankind, though
that is problem enough. The nub of the problem is that
the growth is greatest where the development of the
nations is least: where agriculture and technology are
most primitive. If you think of the world in 2000 AD, of
every hundred people fifty-eight will be Asian; thirteen
will be African; ten will be Latin American; only nine
European; five North American and five Russian.

For most of England's past the world will have seemed
primarily a Western world, but in the present and the
future it is and will be overwhelmingly Asian. (There
are, for instance, over 1000 million in China alone.) And
hunger, and severe malnutrition, will be the continuous
lot of millions. Even now, 460 million people in the world
live in that appalling condition. This is the shape of the
Global Village, as I see it. And that is where I *begin* my
thinking about Church and State today.

The form of the Church must surely enable it to relate
to that sort of world. A 'Constantinian Settlement' –

which includes the kind of settlement the Church of England has today, with an automatically privileged position and status, and a peculiar connection to the Crown and representation in the Lords, and so on – betokens to me a Church which is automatically wrong-footed, so to speak, when it comes to serving the world as it is. Population and poverty are the chief factors which shape our world. And it is the world's population and poverty which raise the most acute questions about the shape of the Church today, not least in relation to the State. The Church has first to be the voice of the poor, the voice of the voiceless.

It would be, surely, a cynical theology which said '"We are all one Body," but let no one think that the Church in Britain is going to do anything significant about the poverty of our fellow human beings in, say, India.' We dare not let the Pauline theology of the Body of Christ be mere words, mere rhetoric: 'If one member suffers, all suffer with it.' If that is not true, let us say so, and 'shut up shop' (even such a 'shop' as this!). No true spirituality can be based on illusion.

Again, it would be a cynical theology which said: '"He has made us accepted in the Beloved" – but, of course, that's a purely *spiritual* statement. Materially He has made some high and some lowly and ordered an extreme difference in their estate; so that, for instance, most of His children in Britain will be so strong that they come to three score years and ten, but four out of ten of his Indian children will die before they're five. Sorry: that's the way He has made things: the way things are and ever more shall be.'

There is a level of poverty, the lot of millions, which often makes human life near to animal existence. I have visited one not entirely untypical area of India, for instance, outside Hyderabad, where there was only one tap to a thousand people.

Such poverty, hunger and thirst raises acutely the question of Church and State, for the Church here must evidently be alongside the Third World. No one thinks more highly than I do of the work of Mother Teresa in Calcutta, having had the great privilege of seeing a good deal of it at first hand; but it is curious how highly people can regard Mother Teresa's work and what a low regard they can have for the kind of political and governmental action which is indispensable if the root causes of the distress with which Mother Teresa deals are to be tackled. The feeding of the masses of the world, the family planning, the housing, the hospitals, the education, the sanitation and the roads require sustained and ordered political and governmental action, not simply 'ambulance work', however marvellously and sacrificially that ambulance work is done.

It is not to be thought that Christians can avoid politics in the years that lie ahead. Because we are now, whether we like it or not, more and more a 'global village', and because we claim as Christians to be 'all one Body', we have to advocate wherever we stand in the world the kind of political decisions which will radically affect the lives of the hungry of the world in, for instance, Asia and Africa. It is easy enough to sit in England or the USA and take up, for instance, an 'anti-Communist' stance, but we have to think, as part of our Christian spirituality, of the kind of government that the masses of the people of India and China require. Then we have to advocate as Christians the kind of government within our own nation which will most help our fellow human beings on the other side of the world: which will help them to survive and bring them a tolerable and just standard of living. As I have travelled about the world, in country after country I have been brought face to face with, for instance, the crying need for reform of land ownership if food production is to be increased. A Church which is not free to proclaim that fact, because it is tied to the powers that be, is a woefully limited Church.

It was Archbishop William Temple who said: 'Justice is

the first expression of love. It is not something contrary to love which love mitigates and softens. It is the first expression of it that must be satisfied before the other and higher expressions find their places.' And the Church has to ask for and press for justice.

It is perhaps worth reflecting that in the last twenty-five years the less developed countries of the world have progressed socially and economically at an unprecedented rate in history, but many of those achievements – in education, feeding, and so on – have been swept away like sandcastles before the advancing tide of population. If the world's population, poverty and hunger shape that society to which the Church must relate, and shape the form of the Church, then the Church will be inextricably involved in politics that will often be unlikely to commend themselves to the government in power, locally and nationally.

And it is because of population, poverty and hunger that the Church will be called to talk powerfully on politics and armaments. When I was last in India I was compelled to confront the whole armaments question. At a conference on aid and development I was chairing in Calcutta, Professor Prodipto Roy, Professor of Economics at Katmandu University, Nepal, said: 'If only one tenth of the expenditure on war of just the two superpowers were turned to peace, in ten years we could provide the basic needs of the whole world.' At that time of the Brandt Report, the annual military bill was approaching £270 billion. And, as President Eisenhower said: 'Every gun that is made, every warship launched, every rocket fired, signifies in a final sense a theft from those who hunger and are not fed, from those who are cold and are not clothed.'

What Eisenhower implied has been put even more explicitly in a UNESCO paper: 'The truth is that the nuclear bomb, without being dropped, has in twenty-six years taken its toll of millions of lives, in the deaths of those who would be alive if the resources spent on nuclear weapons had been used to save life.' It was again Eisenhower, of all people – *General* Eisenhower as we thankfully remember him – who also said: 'Some day the demand for disarmament by hundreds of millions, will I hope, become so universal, and so insistent, that no man, no nation, can withstand it.' I myself believe that day must be now. And I believe the Church has to say this powerfully to the State.

It is, of course, impossible and inappropriate for me to go into the whole disarmament question today: the report of *The Church and the Bomb* has inescapably confronted us with that. But, when all has been said that has been said in that debate, I cannot myself escape the feeling that the majority in the General Synod were speaking and voting as part of a Church that still feels itself inseparably wedded to the *West* – that they have hardly begun to take in and take seriously the shape that is emerging to which I've already referred: the 58 per cent Asian, 13 per cent African and only 5 per cent Russian, 5 per cent North American world: that they have hardly begun to wear the poverty of the world on their hearts and minds. It was primarily the voice of the British – Western – Establishment that was heard that day in Church House, in spite of all its genuine desire to be 'impartial'.

But there is one other accompanying fact of population which is shaping the world: urban growth. Of the 2.2 billion predicted population increase in the final quarter of this century, almost half will live in cities – in developing countries. By the year 2000, ten developing-country cities will have populations of more than 12 million, with Mexico City heading the list at 31 million; and nearly 400 cities will have populations of more than a million – double the present number. The cities which are growing faster now are Bandung, Lagos, Karachi, Bogota, Baghdad, Bangkok and Tehran.

But when the masses of the people reach the cities,

they find always a divided society. India's urban population will increase by 141 per cent in the years between 1975 and 2000. But, as in all major cities in the less-developed countries, over 30 per cent of the population are now slum dwellers or squatters, and there is little chance of that situation being radically changed in the immediate future.

Britain, of course, has had a long time to come to terms with the population explosion, which hit us in the nineteenth century; but, even if we would, we have not been able to escape the effects of membership of that world society in which that explosion still goes on – not least because of our Empire and, later, Commonwealth, involvement. It is helpful to see the migration of, for instance, Commonwealth peoples to our shores in the last twenty-five years – creating a multifaith as well as a multiracial society – as the movement of people under the pressures of the population explosion. In 1951 0.2 per cent of our 49 million population was non-white; by AD 2000 6.7 per cent of our 54 million population will be non-white. (And a multifaith society has something to say about the 'established' religion.) It is also helpful to see some of the West's present employment problems as the result of such cheap labour being available in, for instance, densely populous Asia.

What is now very clear is that the cities of our *own* land will increasingly bear the marks of extreme riches and poverty which are to be seen at their most extreme in places like Calcutta, Mexico City and Lagos. Our divided society will of course have its divisions greatly exacerbated by the unemployment which is following in the wake of the technological revolution which is now upon us. At the time of the riots in Toxteth last year, the constituencies of Toxteth and Scotland-Exchange had, between them, the most intense unemployment problem of any inner-city area in England or Wales. Out of 24,600 men available for work in those areas of

Liverpool, 8,700 (35 per cent) were without jobs; but that was four times the unemployment rate of Crosby, Liverpool.

There are few who see any great prospect of decrease in unemployment in the foreseeable future. And the question now *within our own land* is similar to the question I put earlier concerning the Church and the Third World: will the Church stand by and see Britain become two nations or will she strive to lead the nation to be one caring and compassionate society bearing one another's burdens? In a relatively affluent society, can an *established* Church also be a Church that is 'with the poor and mean and lowly'?

Can an established Church follow where Christ has led, in the years of mass unemployment, and therefore of poverty, that almost certainly lie ahead? In 1977, official government figures showed that over 2 million people in Great Britain had an income below the official minimum. These were the poorest of the poor, the majority of whom were elderly people, sick and disabled, one-parent families supported by low-wage earners; others were unemployed. The 1982 figures show a very large increase in the number of the poor – 6 million men, women and children living on incomes at or below the level of supplementary benefit, and this number will go on increasing for the foreseeable future.

The question is, whether those who are in work, and therefore 'in the money', choose to 'pass by on the other side', and not simply to pass by, but increasingly to opt out of the financing of a good health service, housing, social services and education for all, and whether we go on putting the clock back – as we seem to be doing – to a two-nation society. (May I say that the recent Budget yet again gave more to the rich than to the poor). 'With the poor' need to be three words branded on the Christian heart and mind in the years ahead. And if they are, can the Church retain the form of establishment?

When I was ordained thirty years ago it was already

clear that the Church had not 'lost the cities, but had never had them' – not since the Industrial Revolution; but now the parochial system, which used to be one of the chief glories of the establishment in England, has virtually broken down in vast tracts of its most populous cities, and if the insights into the relation of the Gospel to the Church that are summed up succinctly in the title of the recently published book by David Sheppard, the Bishop of Liverpool, *Bias to the Poor*, are accepted as fundamental, the Church of England must make haste to experiment with, and develop, forms of ministry and mission to the poorest and most deprived areas of our land which will make it anything but an established Church. But the question is whether the legal shackles of the establishment will allow and encourage such experiment.

It would be interesting to know, for instance, in the recent controversial appointment to this hugely important See of London, what were the Prime Minister's priorities: whether it was to find the man best equipped to help the clergy and people – of Stepney, Tower Hamlets and Poplar, of Paddington and Notting Hill – to be responsive to the Gospel.

I have come myself to believe that it is of the essence of the Church that it be a 'confessional' Church. When the Church aspires to the political and social power the Constantinian 'Settlement' gave it, I believe, with Bishop Lesslie Newbigin, that it aspires to an 'illegitimate syncretism'. I believe with Fr. Benson, the founder of the Cowley Fathers, that 'when Constantine took up the Cross, the Church laid it down.'

The alternative to establishment is not, as some have suggested, to be a sect. Indeed, I believe an establishment itself can justifiably be called a particular kind of sect posing as other than it is – as, for instance, with most of the nation no longer belonging to it, the Church of England as *the* Church of England. (Since 1930 the number of Roman Catholics in this country has grown from 6.6 per cent to 11 per cent of the population, far outnumbering the 1¾ million on the electoral rolls of the Church of England.)

I do not want to belong to a sect, if by that is meant an intellectual or ecclesiastical or pietistic ghetto. Nor do I imagine the Church can ever be a kind of 'pure' body that lives by absolutes whilst the rest of the world gets on with its compromising life. The Church, wherever it is, has to discover the relative merits of justice and freedom and to commit itself to action on behalf of that which is relatively better. And as William Blake said: 'He who would do good to another must do it in minute particulars.'

Yet there are some absolutes, some masts to which the Church has to nail itself. An example, I think, is the colour bar. There is no way in which a Christian can compromise on that – though there will be some ambiguous situations that arise as one works out loyalty to that absolute. A priest in South Africa once said to me: 'If I open my mouth I shall be sent back to Britain. If I keep silent, there's no point in my staying.' Nor can I ever forget how Dietrich Bonhoeffer scandalised some by regarding as a mere bagatelle the raising of his arm to give the Hitler salute. 'This thing isn't worth dying for,' he said. In every situation compromise ethics operate to some extent.

Here in England, the relation between Church and State does not come anywhere near to demanding our suffering and death as it does in so many places around the globe at the moment. We must be thankful for that. Yet I hold the conviction that in the years ahead, if the Church is to be the Church, it will, from time to time, by its very adherence to the Gospel, be a cause of scandal. It must be liberated, freed, to be able to be a cause of scandal – for the sake of the Gospel.

The Gospel. I need to return to the Gospel before I end, for in the end, the relation between Church and State most of all needs to be one in which the Church does not 'do homage' to the State – I choose the phrase carefully – simply because the message of Jesus was about Kingship and the nature of that Kingship; about the universal sovereignty of God. In its universality, the Church transcends our tribal and national parochialities. In its sovereignty, the Church speaks of the priority of Jesus over the emperor and sets an inevitable collision course between them from time to time: it is set on an inevitable collision course with the imperial power of Rome, Moscow, Pretoria, Jerusalem, Washington and 10 Downing Street – indeed, with all 'earthly powers'. Yet those 'earthly powers' are themselves called to be the revelation of the creating and redeeming love of God, and the Church is to help them to be so.

In my earlier years, my own views on Church and State were much influenced by Archbishop William Temple. I remember with gratitude his book, *Citizen and Churchman*, which went over the reasons why he had gone back on his earlier views on Church and State. In 1913 it was clear that he was for disestablishment; by the time he wrote *Citizen and Churchman* – 1941 – his earlier convictions had suffered a complete bouleversement.

I think I must be open and honest and say that it is because, in so many places in the world at large, I have seen the governing power defending the way of life of the privileged few, and the Church assisting that defence, and in so few places have I seen the Church able to enter into, for instance, the Marxist-Christian dialogue – which I now believe to be essential – that I have gone back on my earlier views on Church and State.

I conclude what I have to say by underlining that population, poverty and hunger are the dominant facts of the world society; the response of nearly one third of the earth to those facts is to pay homage to the teachings of confrontation, and dialogue between the two is an absolute demand of history in our time, a demand which is rendered more exigent by the fact that it is now technologically possible to destroy, in the name of rival ideologies, every trace of life on earth.

Many Marxists no longer view religion as an opiate and recognise it as an expression of the highest aspirations of the human personality. Many Christians – I take as an example the present Norris-Hulse Professor of Divinity in the University of Cambridge, Nicholas Lash, a Catholic lay theologian and philosopher – are beginning to see the necessity of dialogue, not just in theology and philosophy, but acting together to contribute to the transformation of human existence.

For me, the disestablishment of the Church of England is now an important step towards getting into a position to be able to help the world that Marx sought to help: the world of God's poor.

CHRISTIAN RESPONSIBILITY IN POLITICS

David Steel

8 Christian Responsibility in Politics

by David Steel

I realise that I am one of the few speakers in this series who is not a member of the Church of England – I am in fact an elder of the Church of Scotland. I don't think, therefore, that there would be much point in my talking to you about the more arcane points of the establishment of the Church of England because I don't know very much about them myself – they are not a matter of absorbing interest to me. What is, however, of absorbing interest to me is the interconnection of a person's religious faith with their secular vocation, for to me the two are inextricably interwoven.

Now of course I am a politician, and a party one, and I became one partly because I believed that my Christian faith was increasingly calling me to this. And it is precisely because I want to speak and live as a Christian that if, in the course of this talk, I criticise people or attitudes, I do so not because I want to score any party-political points, but because these attitudes seem to me a gross distortion of the Christian faith. I am not claiming for my own party any flawlessness in this area. As I heard my 'alter ego', Nadir Dinshaw, observe in a talk which he gave here eighteen months ago, 'the Liberal Party is not exactly the earthly incarnation of the

Communion of Saints,' and I am well aware of the truth of this statement.

The commonest distortion, I suppose, and it is one that never ceases to enrage me, is the smug sentiment, usually uttered by comfortable people sitting comfortably in their homes, that the Church should not involve itself in politics, by which they mean that the Church should never seek to change, but merely defend the status quo, a status quo which of course is highly advantageous to them. Now this is a wholly untenable argument, for a number of reasons.

Firstly, it goes against the whole spirit of the Incarnation and the Gospel. For our Lord Himself, in His own prayer, commanded us to ask for our daily bread, and to pray that God's Kingdom may come *on earth*, as it is in heaven – so much for the apostles of that heretical Gospel, who love to castigate Christians with social consciences as being 'too concerned with the Third World and not enough with the next world', a sub-Christian and un-Christian sentiment which can best be answered, I think, by one of the greatest souls of all time, Christian or non-Christian, Mahatma Gandhi, himself an ascetic of the most austere kind, who said: 'To a hungry man, God Himself would hesitate to appear, except in the shape of food.'

Then, even before the actual birth of Our Lord, Mary had prophesied what God wished to do through His Son whom she was to bear: 'He hath filled the hungry with good things, and the rich He hath sent empty away, He hath put down the mighty from their seats, and hath exalted the humble and meek.' Surely that is highly political language, and it is little wonder that Bernard Shaw said that the Magnificat was more revolutionary than the Internationale, that Thomas Hancock should call it the 'Hymn of the Universal Social Revolution', that according to Dante, Robert, King of Sicily, ordered it to be sung only in Latin, and that for the same reason it is today banned in several South American countries, as being too subversive.

Yet even the Pope tells the Roman Catholic priests of South America that they must have nothing to do with politics, whilst he vigorously supports the Roman Catholic hierarchy and priests of his own native Poland, who are, rightly, in the forefront of the heroic struggle for human rights and human dignity. Churchmen may themselves feel called to politics. The foreign minister of Nicaragua at present is a Catholic priest. And for myself, it is a source of great pride that a Church of Scotland minister, the Rev. Geoffrey Shaw, a member of the Labour Party, gave his life to outstanding pastoral and political work, initially in the Gorbals, and then as chairman of the whole Strathclyde Regional Council.

And this hypocrisy is compounded when no similar words of criticism are uttered when one of the senior bishops of the Church of England attended and spoke at a recent conference on Christianity and Conservatism (described by a fellow MP as a contradiction in terms, a sentiment with which I have great sympathy). Yet, when an outstanding churchman like Archbishop Huddleston rightly opposed certain Conservative attitudes on Africa, he was viciously attacked by Conservative Christians, who ought to have known better.

Nevertheless, strangely enough, two of the greatest English saints – St. Thomas Becket, and St. Thomas More, one an Archbishop, the other Lord Chancellor, both great Christians, both politicians – defied the temporal power of the State, were both martyred, and are both duly honoured today for their defiance and their martyrdom. And it is well for the Church to remember this in the present illiberal climate of opinion which is such a great danger to truly Christian values. For how, in the complex world of today, when vicarious almsgiving can but scratch the surface of human need and human despair, are we to love our neighbour as ourselves? How are we to make even the most marginal reparation, the smallest gestures of effective caring except by political methods – by a more just social and economic system in our nation and in the world? Our neighbour was defined by Christ as someone who does *us* good even though we have exploited, rejected and scorned him.

But what utter humbug this is anyway – the very Constitution of this country demands that twenty-six senior bishops of the Church of England *must by law* sit in the House of Lords, thereby forming part of the political process of government. How do these same critics then reconcile this fact with their objection? Does this make them political priests? Only if they dare to apply the Gospel to social issues, for as Dr. Kenneth Slack says: 'In my forty years of ministry I have never heard the expression "political priest" applied to a right-wing figure.' To them, the Church must not depart from right-wing ideology, or disagree with the reactions of a right-wing government – so Archbishop Ramsay was criticised for even suggesting that it might be legitimate to use force to put down rebellion against the Crown in Rhodesia, as it then was, and Archbishop Runcie for his Falkland Islands sermon at St. Paul's, when he refused to join in the triumphalist jingoism the government wanted.

What such people really want is the sort of Church, obedient to their dictates, as is the Church in Russia. For instance, the Prime Minister and various members of her party are busy opposing unilateral nuclear disarmament by comparisons with the rise of Nazism in Germany in the 1930s. One does not have to be a unilateralist, and I myself am not one, to know how spurious this argument is, as far as this country is concerned, and how dangerous. For by doing this she is very cleverly drawing attention away from the true comparison, which is with conditions in this country at present and in the Germany of the early 1930s. Remember that Hitler was democratically elected to power, as our governments are, that the Germans were, and have become again, a civilised cultured people, but that they, nevertheless, identified a certain section of society, the Jews, as the cause of their economic and social ills. All too sadly many people in this country already do so with coloured people.

The post-war Germans then acquiesced in inhuman legislation against the scapegoats they had themselves created, as we have done ever since 1968; their politicians, like many of ours, made racialism (a cardinal blasphemy against the Christian faith) respectable; their own liberties were then eroded, as ours will be if the proposed Police and Evidence Bill is passed in its present form, until – so far, thank God, unlike us – it ended in Auschwitz, Buchenwald and the martyrdom of dissidents like Bonhoeffer. Of course we have not got there, but before we become too complacent, let us not forget that even the Churches, with the marvellous exception of the Confessing Church, became complaisant and pliable tools of the State.

So it is on the Churches in this country, while there is yet time, that a heavy responsibility now rests. Is the established Church going to tolerate legislation that empowers the police to take away files or records, of however confidential a nature, thereby striking at the very roots of a vital part of their priestly ministry? The Churches *must* unite in opposition to this and many clauses of the Bill – those Conservative MPs who claim to be Christians *must* be made to see the inconsistency of professing that faith and voting for this Bill. I attach no value to the argument, plausibly advanced by some Church leaders, that Christianity must concern itself with the articles of faith, and that on many other matters, it is legitimate for Christians to hold different views.

How *can* it be legitimate for Christians to hold different views on apartheid, on racialism, on torture, on the erosion of civil liberties, especially for the most vulnerable and underprivileged members of our society? Even 3,000 years ago people knew better than this – let me quote you some favourite lines of mine from the Book of Leviticus: 'When an alien settles in your land, you should not oppress him. He shall be treated as a native born among you, and you shall love him as a man like yourself because you were aliens in Egypt. I am the Lord your God.' That was hardly the spirit that motivated the Immigration Acts of 1968, 1971, and more recently the squalid debate in the House of Commons on the pitifully small number of Asian husbands and fiances who come to Britain. I was appalled to read an article advocating compulsory repatriation, very cleverly worded in academic language, which appeared in the journal of a group of influential Conservatives.

I welcome with all my heart, therefore, the protest made by so many Anglican bishops against the Police and Criminal Evidence Bill, and I should like to emphasise again that I am not making a party-political point – were an Alliance or Labour government to introduce such a Bill, I hope that the same bishops would protest, and succeed in getting these extremely offensive clauses of the Bill squashed; for the Church must be fearless in proclaiming the Gospel, regardless of whichever party is in power – politics are ephemeral, God alone is eternal; yet it is by the ephemeral that we shall be judged for our fitness for the eternal.

The Church should be demanding that politicians tackle the social issues underlying the present crime wave, notably unemployment, rather than expecting our police to use draconian powers to put out the fires we have lit by our own failure. In this, the centenary year of his birth, I cannot find better words to describe this aspect of the Church's duty than those used by a man who was perhaps the greatest bishop the Church of England has produced in this century. Writing in the *Fortnightly Review* in November 1939, two months after the beginning of the Second World War, George Bell, Bishop of Chichester, said:

> So when all the resources of the State are concentrated, for example, on winning a war, the Church is not a part of these resources... It possesses an authority independent of the State. It is bound because of that authority to proclaim the realities which outlast change. It has to preach the Gospel of redemption ... it is not the State's spiritual auxiliary, with exactly the same ends as the State. To give the impression that it is, is both to do a profound disservice to the nation, and to betray its own principles.

Surely these prophetic and courageous words speak never more clearly to our condition than they do today, and they are words which the Church must constantly reiterate, and to which the State *must* listen.

Although I am frequently very critical of my own profession, I fear that the Church's own record on human rights has been far from perfect – many bishops supported slavery because to abolish it would have harmed the rights of property, which, according to them, was inherent in the Christian gospel; a strange view to hold for followers of a man who had nowhere to lay his head. Far too often the Church has compromised with the temporal power, has sought refuge in plausible evasions, and spoke with a muted and qualified voice, if it has spoken at all. It has ignored or stifled its own prophets when alive, and then hastened to take credit for them, once they have died. As the Rev. Kenneth Leech said in this church last year – this church, which under its marvellously radical, truly Christian Rector, affirms Christianity's concern with the whole of humanity:

> The Church must change, must cease to be afraid of the principalities and powers, and repent of its past. It must see in anger and revolt the signs of God's presence, and God's justice. It must abandon its role of social control, and defence of established structures, if it is to become a sign of hope and justice for the City and its people.

Yet finally may I refer you back once again to some words of Bishop Bell, which appear to me to be the epitome of Christian discipleship and Christian involvement and which are perhaps especially relevant to members of my profession:

> To despair of being able to do anything, or to refuse to do anything, is to be guilty of infidelity, just as to be the cause of men becoming refugees is to sin against the Almighty. For it is in the civil order and in the actualities of daily life that the Christian's decisions are made. The Gospel is relevant to the whole of human conduct. Christianity requires action which has to be taken in conditions of actual life.

So I hope and believe that the Church that produced George Bell and Charles Gore, Trevor Huddleston and Colin Winter, will not fail to rise to the challenge which now faces it.

THE FREEDOM OF THE GOSPEL

Mark Santer

9 The Freedom of the Gospel

Mark Santer

Seventy years ago – that is, before the First World War –
a book was published called *Churches in the Modern State*. It
was admired and used by Laski, and it is still worth
reading, not least because it is highly readable. The
author was John Neville Figgis, a Cambridge political
historian who had become a Mirfield father.

'A Free Church in a Free State' is the title of the first
chapter. Figgis raises questions which are with us still,
and I want to use his discussion as my starting-point in
thinking today about the freedom of the Gospel, and the
freedom of the Church as servant of the Gospel.

He begins by 'discussing what we mean by claiming
freedom for the Church' (page 4). For him the basic
question is this. Is the Church, or any Church, a body
with an inherent life of its own, with its own power of
self-development and self-expression, a body therefore
to be *recognised* by the State? Or is it to be seen in the end
as a creation of the State, existing only on terms
determined by the State and incapable, except by decree
of the State, of varying those terms? He makes it quite
clear that this is a question which affects *all* Churches;
'establishment' as such is a side-issue; also that it is a
question affecting not only the Churches but all other
communities within society – such as trade unions

(hence Laski's interest), colleges and professional bodies. Do such bodies have a life of their own, or only a life conceded to them by the sovereign State?

Figgis asserts forcibly that Churches and other communal bodies have an inherent life of their own. But he is aware that this fact is not evident to all. Politicians and lawyers have a bias, he says, towards State absolutism, grounded at bottom in the traditions of Roman Law, which see all authority as derived from the sovereign. As an extreme example he quotes the French secularist politician Emile Combes: 'There are, there can be, no rights except the right of the State, and there are, and there can be, no other authority than the authority of the Republic' (page 56). This is how, on pages 99-100 of his book, Figgis sums up this part of his argument:

> We have seen that the essential minimum of any claim we make for the Church must depend on its recognition as a social union with an inherent original power of self-development, acting as a person with a mind and will of its own. All other matters between Church and State are questions of detail; and there is room for mutual concession. What is not a detail but a principle is that which I have put forward, and we have seen that this is not granted; that it is opposed by the prevailing opinion of State omnipotence entrenched in popular thought, and still more so in the opinion of lawyers... Further, we have seen that this false conception of the State as the only true political entity apart from the individual is at variance not only with ecclesiastical liberty, but with the freedom of all other communal life, and ultimately with that of the individual...

Although it is more than seventy years since Figgis wrote those words, the issues are not dead. Anyone can see this who observes and reflects on the views held

112

today as a matter of course by many politicians about the sovereignty of Parliament, or on the attitudes often taken towards the Churches (and the Church of England in particular) and towards trade unions.

Establishment as such, said Figgis, is not the basic issue. He is right. What is at issue is the particular form of the relationship which exists, or is believed to exist, between a particular State and a particular Church. If 'establishment' is a problem for the Church of England, as Figgis believed seventy years ago (and as I believe today), this is not because it can be called 'establishment', but because of the particular institutional structures of the relationship between the State and the Church of England, and because of the habits of mind and behaviour which they foster both in statesmen and in churchmen.

There are four areas where I believe our particular arrangements are bad; bad either because they obscure the true nature of the Church and therefore of the Gospel, or because they corrupt the mind of the Church.

1 There is the matter of appointments. It is plainly wrong that the chief pastors of the flock of Christ, the successors of the Apostles, should be appointed by the Crown. Whether the Crown be the Queen herself, or the Queen as advised by her Prime Minister, or the Queen as advised by the Prime Minister after consultation with the Church, makes no essential difference. Christ entrusted the care and leadership of his Church to his apostles. He did not go on to entrust the care and appointment of their successors to the Emperor Tiberius or to Pontius Pilate as his local representative. The State's interest in religion, now as always, is in the end that it should help to keep the people quiet. The State's interest in religion is not in the end that the Gospel should be preached and lived.

So I am not content with the present arrangements for episcopal appointments. I do not object only to the fact that the Prime Minister is seen as free to choose between two names submitted to her, or else to send them back and ask for more. Nor do I object only to the fact that these arrangements are seen as a discretionary concession which can in principle be withdrawn. I object still more to the fact that the Church acquiesces in such a view. And I object most of all to the fact that the Crown, in any sense, has the last word. If – as we were told in 1976 when the present arrangements were agreed on – giving the Prime Minister the last word in episcopal appointments is the price we must pay for having bishops in the House of Lords, the price is too high. The Church must be free, and be seen to be free, to choose her own pastors. Otherwise their authority is seen to rest on foundations other than and additional to those of Christ and his apostles; and that, in effect, is a denial of the sufficiency of Christ as the only foundation and authority for our apostolic ministry.

2 The chief act of the English Reformation, from a constitutional point of view, was the subordination to the Crown of all ecclesiastical authority for the making of liturgy, the determination of doctrine, and the formulation and administration of ecclesiastical law. The canons of the Church of England, as recently revised, still speak of the Church of England as 'established according to the laws of this realm under the Queen's Majesty' (A1) and say further that 'we acknowledge that the Queen's most excellent Majesty, acting according to the laws of the realm, is the highest power under God in this kingdom, and has supreme authority over all persons in all causes, as well ecclesiastical as civil' (A7).

But when a minister of the United Reformed Church is ordained or instituted he is asked to deny precisely this. Following the Presbyterian tradition, he declares his assent to the following proposition: 'We declare that the Lord Jesus Christ, the only King and head of the Church, has therein appointed a government distinct from civil government and in things spiritual not subordinate thereto...'

As far as the Church of England is concerned, it is too easily assumed that, for instance, the General Synod deliberates and legislates not only by *permission* or *consent* of the Queen in Parliament, but also by *delegation* from the Queen in Parliament. If one looks at the recent parliamentary debates on the protection of the Book of Common Prayer, one will see that politician after politician, and peer after peer, takes it for granted that the Church's synods have a merely delegated authority, an authority whose limits are determined by statute, and an authority which can in principle be withdrawn. In other words, the General Synod is seen as analogous to a minister of the Crown in his delegated capacity to make administrative orders for factories or immigration regulations, and the Church courts are viewed like administrative tribunals.

I object to this strongly. But I object still more to the fact that churchmen tacitly accept this way of seeing things. What we need to recover is the sense that the synods of the Church have an inherent authority of their own, resting not on the say-so of the Crown or of Parliament, but upon the baptism and ordination of the people who compose them. 'Where two or three are gathered together in my name, there am I in the midst of them' (Matt. 18:20). That, among other things, is a political statement about the authority of the synods and tribunals of the Church. For myself, I think it a pity that the bishops and clergy do not wear liturgical dress in the General Synod, as they used to in the Convocations. To wear the same dress in assembly for deliberation as in assembly for prayer would make an important symbolic point, that whether praying or deliberating, a synod of the Church is a liturgical assembly, convoked by the

Holy Spirit, under the rule, in the end, not of the Queen of England but of Christ crucified and risen.

3   If the powers exercised by the Church are viewed as merely concessionary, it naturally follows that their exercise is seen as bound by the terms of the concession. Yet that is the principle which underlies the Worship and Doctrine Measure of 1974. By the law of the realm, the Book of Common Prayer remains permanently available for use, and its forms of service cannot be altered or superseded without the approval of Parliament. All other forms of service are no more than 'alternatives'. All doctrine and liturgy in the Church of England is to be determined by reference to the Book of Common Prayer of 1662 and the Thirty-Nine Articles.

Quite apart from the ecumenical embarrassment of letting ourselves be thus legally and permanently tied to particular formulae which are inherently transient, it is in principle wrong that the doctrine and liturgy of the Church should be, in the end, determinable not by the living voice of the Church but by reference to the dead hand of documents legally interpreted.

One may contrast not only the sense of the living authority of the Holy Spirit in the Roman Catholic Church but also, once again, the words to which a minister of the United Reformed Church must give his assent:

> It is the duty of the Church, under the authority of Holy Scripture and in corporate responsibility to Jesus Christ its ever-living head, to be open at all times to the leading of the Holy Spirit. The Church therefore has the right to make such new declarations of faith, and for such purposes, as may from time to time be required by obedience to the same Spirit.

The Methodist Church can issue a new Service Book.

The Roman Catholic Church can issue a new Missal. The Church of England is denied authority to issue a new Prayer Book; the best it can manage is 'alternatives'.

In my judgment, the terms of the Worship and Doctrine Measure show that, in principle, a battle still has to be won: the battle for the recognition of the Church's inherent spiritual authority for the ordering of her own affairs not, at the end of the day, with reference to the British Crown and Parliament, but with reference to the whole Catholic and Apostolic Church of Christ.

4 I referred earlier to the habits of mind and behaviour which are fostered by the Church of England's relationship with the State. The institutional arrangements under which anyone operates condition the way he thinks. So I am worried less by the fact that statesmen and politicians claim powers to which they are not entitled, as by the fact that churchmen cheerfully and unthinkingly concede the claims.

The worst thing about the special status of the Church of England is the corruption of the spirit which it encourages. We collude, implicitly, with the notion that 'Anglican' equals 'really English', thereby reducing our fellow-Christians to the status of inferior citizens. We may not feel it; they do. The case is still worse when we think of the place of other non-Christian communities in England. We quite like being nice to them. What would we feel like if we had to feel grateful for their patronage?

Another consequence of establishment is the way our leaders feel constrained, not by any external bonds, but by the internal bonds which they have accepted, not to step too far out of line. Whether one likes it or not, one feels a natural sense of obligation to people who give one jobs. Yet why should a bishop have to justify himself, or be congratulated as if it were something surprising, if in the name of the Gospel he speaks out for the cause of peace or justice? It is the spirit of servility and snobbery

in the Church itself which is the most evil fruit of
establishment. As always, our internal bonds are much
stronger than any external constraint. But you can't
entirely separate the two. For the external constraints
provide the soil in which the internal bonds grow.

The Church of England suffers fatally from its
residual identification with English society as a whole. It
is fatal, because it is illusory. If we have a responsibility
to society as a whole, that must be because of our
obedience to the Gospel, not because of any particular
pretensions. Here (from pages 133-134 of his book) is
one more passage from Figgis. He makes the point
forcibly:

> We cannot escape sectarianism even by sacrificing
> the creeds; still less by attempting a wholly unreal
> identification of the Church with the nation, an
> identification which had ceased to represent all the
> facts even in the time of Hooker, and has been
> becoming less true ever since. Neither, on the other
> hand, in such a world can you without disaster
> attempt to impose the standards of the Church on
> the whole mass of your countrymen, except in so
> far as they still rule in some matters on other
> grounds. Every attempt to raise the code of the
> nation to that of the Church leads, if unsuccessful,
> to an attempt to lower the code of the Church to
> that of the world, because it proceeds from a notion
> that at bottom the two are identical. Thus if the lax
> party gets the upper hand it will compel the Church
> to conform to its standards, an attempt which is
> being made on all hands just now. The two societies
> are distinct – distinct in origin, in aim, and (if you
> have toleration) in personnel. The smaller is never
> likely, as things are, to control the larger. If she
> attempts to do so she will be beaten, and in the
> process be like to lose her own freedom ... It is the
> essence of the Church to be different from the

world, and her mission to proclaim that difference. Whenever men try to sanctify the world by raising it to the level of the Church, they commonly succeed only in lowering the life of the Church to accommodate it to the practice of the world.

If as Christians we are to find our true freedom, then we must be clear about our true identity. This sends us back to a number of basic texts in the New Testament: 'Pay to Caesar what is due to Caesar, and pay God what is due to God' (Matt. 22:21). What is due to Caesar? Taxes. What is due to God? Yourself. 'My kingdom', says Jesus to Pilate, 'does not belong to this world' (John 18:36). No, it transcends and judges this world. 'We,' says St. Paul, 'are citizens of heaven, and from heaven we expect our deliverer to come, the Lord Jesus Christ' (Phil. 3:20).

This was what most upset the Roman authorities about Christians: the sense that, at the end of the day, they belonged elsewhere. This is also what has upset Englishmen in thinking about Roman Catholics. They have another loyalty, one which is not ultimately subject to England. Thomas More made the point on the scaffold, protesting that he died the king's good servant, but God's first. The issue comes out movingly and simply in the account of the martyrdom of some North African peasants in the late second century.

The governor, Saturninus, said: 'If you begin to malign our sacred rites, I shall give you no hearing. Swear instead by the genius of our Lord the Emperor.'

Speratus replied: 'I do not recognise the empire of this world. Rather, I serve that God whom no man has seen nor can see with these eyes. I have not stolen, and on whatever I buy I pay the tax, because I recognise my Lord, who is Emperor of kings and of all nations.'

The governor said to the others: 'Cease to be of this persuasion.'

One of them answered: 'We have no one else to fear

except *our* Lord who is in heaven.'

Another one, a woman, joined in: 'Honour to Caesar as Caesar; but fear to God' (*Acts of the Scillitan Martyrs*).

That brings out a fundamental point. Whom in the end do we *fear*? What, at the end of the day, are we afraid of losing? In the Gospel Jesus says to his friends, that is, to those who trust him and belong to him: 'Do not fear those who kill the body and after that have nothing more they can do. I will warn you who to fear: fear him who, after he has killed, has authority to cast into hell. Believe me, he is the one to fear.' But then he continues: 'Are not sparrows five for twopence? And yet not one of them is overlooked by God. More than that, even the hairs of your head have all been counted. So have no fear; you are worth more than any number of sparrows.'

So no one else has power to destroy us, and God himself, who has the power to do so, won't. Who then can destroy us? Only ourselves. This becomes clear from the Lord's very next words. 'I tell you this: everyone who acknowledges me before men, the Son of Man will acknowledge before the angels of God; but he who disowns me will be disowned before the angels of God' (Luke 12: 4-9).

The Lord will not abandon us. We are as free as our faith gives us strength to be. That is what we learn from the stories of the martyrs, right down to our own day. Those who have their treasure in heaven have nothing to lose on earth which God will not restore to them a thousandfold.

The freedom we are talking about is the freedom of Jesus Christ, the freedom we see paradoxically displayed in the story of the passion. 'The Father loves me, because I lay down my life, to receive it back again. No one has robbed me of it; I am laying it down of my own free will' (John 10:17f). Above all in St. John's account of the passion, although Jesus is the prisoner, bound and powerless, the obvious victim of other men's actions, He remains the lord and master of it all. The roles of Pilate and Jesus are strangely reversed, as in the great East window of King's College Chapel in Cambridge, where Pilate the judge sits beneath the foot of the cross on which hangs the crucified prisoner.

Let us return briefly to Church and State. The institutional arrangements matter because of their effects on people's minds and actions: I have no doubt of that. But they are secondary. What is primary is the quality of our union with Christ, as it expresses itself in prayer and in action – action which must include the transformation of the institutional arrangements. The Lord whom we are called to follow is the poor, humble and crucified Jesus, Jesus on his way to his death. Those who follow him are called to carry their own cross, the instrument of their own execution. That is *our* task. We can leave it to God, as Jesus did, to look after the resurrection.

All our human love of glory, all our clinging to power and privilege, all of our fear of letting go, come down in the end to fear of death and lack of faith in *God's* power to look after us. Our task is to follow the Lord, and trust to God to look after the consequences. Christian freedom is rooted in Christian faith: the faith that God will not fail himself.

'Here', says St. Paul 'are some words you may trust' – and if we are not prepared to apply them as much to our institutional life as to our so-called 'personal' life, then we have not heard what he is saying –

> Here are some words you may trust:
> If we died with him, we shall live with him.
> If we endure, we shall reign with him.
> If we deny him, he will deny us.
> If we are faithless, he keeps faith,
>   for he cannot deny himself (2 Tim. 2: 11–13).

Tony Castle

The Hodder Book of
Christian Quotations

This inspiring collection of quotations, comprising
the ancient and the modern, English and American,
Protestant and Catholic, is an invaluable source of
reference and spiritual nourishment.

Quotations by over a thousand authors are
included, illustrating the thoughts, ideas and
aspirations of men and women down the ages.

'The variety of quotations, from the most un-
expected sources, is astonishing. Many, as I read,
struck a deep chord and caused me to think afresh.'
Georgette Butcher

Os Guinness

The Gravedigger File

What can explain the virtual collapse of the European Church? Or the vital change in American Christianity so that it can be dismissed as 'privately engaging but socially irrelevant'? How is it that Protestantism has come full circle, itself in need of reformation?

Secret papers reveal that these problems are not accidental nor unrelated, but the work of Operation Gravedigger, a sinister design to sabotage Western Christianity.

Beginning in a misty Oxford square, the story moves to its climax on a modern Damascus road, bringing into sharp focus the challenge to Christian discipleship in the late twentieth century.

Hugh T Kerr & John M Mulder

Conversions

A fascinating and unique collection of personal conversion accounts which span all of Christian history. Fifty well-known Christians, from the Apostle Paul and St Augustine to Simone Weil and Charles Colson, describe their own conversion to Christianity.

William A Heth &
Gordon J Wenham

Jesus and Divorce

For centuries, the Church has been the foremost
authority on marriage, but divergent views among
Christians are passionately held. The authors of
this meticulously researched study believe that a
new look at Christ's words is now essential to
enable an honest reassessment of their interpretation and application.

Each view is analysed in full and detailed attention
is given to the near consensus that remarriage after
divorce is allowable on the grounds of immorality.

JESUS AND DIVORCE is a major and far-reaching
contribution to the divorce debate.

F F Bruce

Jesus and Christian Origins
Outside the New Testament

What proof outside the New Testament is there for
the historical existence of Jesus Christ?

F F Bruce has studied in detail other historical
records and drawn from a variety of Jewish, pagan,
apocryphal and Islamic writings of the New
Testament period, referring also to the Dead Sea
Scrolls, the Gospel of Thomas and the Koran. Every
important source is considered in the discussion,
and archaeological evidence is taken into full
account.